Christopher Copper-Ind is publisher of *International Investment,* a financial news organization in London. He also writes tailored reports on Turkey and Iran for a Middle East consultancy. Before this he was editorial director of a media company in Istanbul covering the economies of the Middle East and Central Asia. From 2004 to 2010 Copper-Ind was a company director at the publishing house Stacey International, for whom he negotiated contracts across the Middle East and Asia for high-end book projects and business guides.

As a publisher and Middle East consultant, he has worked on projects in over 25 countries. His business trips did not always go according to plan, however. Negotiating for a contract in Iran in 2009, he found himself briefly imprisoned on charges of espionage.

He divides his time between London and Paris.

how to: ACADEMY launched in September 2013. Since then it has organized over 1000 talks and seminars on Business, Lifestyle, and Science & Technology, which have been attended by 100,000 people. The aim of the series is to anticipate the needs of the reader by providing clarity, precision and know-how in an increasingly complex world.

First published 2019 by Bluebird
an imprint of Pan Macmillan
20 New Wharf Road, London N1 9RR
Associated companies throughout the world
www.panmacmillan.com

ISBN 978-1-5098-1463-3

9 8 7 6 5 4 3 2 1

A CIP catalogue record for this book is available from the British Library.

Typeset in 10.5/14 pt Charter ITC Std by Jouve (UK), Milton Keynes
Printed and bound by CPI Group (UK) Ltd, Croydon, CR0 4YY

CHRISTOPHER COPPER-IND

HOW TO: NEGOTIATE

bluebird
books for life

For Lalé

Contents

Introduction: Understanding negotiation 1

1: Power and psychology 17

2: Essential skills 29

3: Know your opponent 42

4: Strategy 51

5: Key stages 63

6: Cultural differences 76

7: The deal 91

8: Conclusions 111

Notes 114

Index 117

Introduction
UNDERSTANDING NEGOTIATION

The most important trip you may take in life is
meeting people half way
– Henry Boye[1]

Heaven prohibits certain pleasures; but one can
generally negotiate a compromise
– Molière, *Tartuffe*, Act IV, scene 5

People often think of negotiation as the art of obtaining what you want: that if you're canny enough, you can negotiate on your own terms to serve your own ends. In the real world, and certainly in the realm of business, this all-conquering, zero-sum interpretation is rarely allowed to play out on its own terms. For in the vast majority of cases, the complex and subtle act of negotiating is, in fact, the art of the middle way. This should not be interpreted as painful self-sacrifice or indeed, for the other party, winner-takes-all glory. Rather, the best kind of negotiation is a process that, taking into account some or all of either side's needs, results in *both* parties feeling they have come away with, for the most part, what they wanted. Put simply, effective negotiation is the art of compromise.

Nonetheless, negotiation is absolutely grounded in knowing what you want before you enter into discussions. Indeed, this is vital. Yet this vision should be tempered both by what you gauge you can realistically achieve and what is deemed reasonable to expect. Negotiation could equally, and accurately, be described as the art of not getting entirely what you want. As we'll see in the following chapters, this involves being alert to what your opponent wants, too.

The aim of this book is, of course, to help you do what it says on the cover. As most readers of *How to Negotiate* will be business people of one sort or another, I'll generally be focusing on that world, and its everyday situations relating to making deals, signing contracts and the like. At times, we'll look more closely at examples of negotiation strategies from within the opaque realm of international diplomacy. This can, of course, involve extreme instances of negotiation, needing extreme levels of compromise (or none at all). Hostage crises, for example, carry huge stakes for the hostages themselves, and call for negotiation skills of the highest order. Most instances of international diplomacy, though, including peace treaties and recent ground-breaking agreements such as the Iran nuclear deal, brokered by America's then Secretary of State John Kerry in 2015, have compromise at their core, even if the cost of failure (war, poverty, economic sanctions, international isolation) has the potential to be much higher than a typical negotiation exchange in an office boardroom, the outcome of which will either be a deal, or no deal.

A life skill

Whatever the setting, be it the kitchen, the school playground (the negotiation instinct starts early), the boardroom or an international peace conference, negotiation is arguably one of life's most important and useful skills. It is central to the success, or otherwise, of almost any business. Successful negotiation has avoided international conflict, court cases and resolved disputes in everything from trade tariffs to marital strife. Negotiation can bring about harmony from discord, has the power to turn stark differences into mutually beneficial agreements and is the unseen skill at work in almost any successful outcome involving two or more parties.

Yet despite its prevalence in almost all areas of our lives, it is also one of the most misunderstood skills, and as such frequently leads to many a missed opportunity. Furthermore, many people actively seek to avoid the often uncomfortable feelings the act of negotiating can evoke. The intensity and cross-examination that come with bargaining can be a stressful experience. The pressure to come away with a valuable contract, while remaining inscrutably calm and level headed throughout, is enough to put off many people before they have even begun.

Learning to negotiate effectively is a lesson in self-awareness. Yet a skilled and informed negotiator will be also acutely attuned to his opponent's priorities: their values, schedule, aims and agenda. The accomplished negotiator is always listening. He is constantly alert to his opponent's motives, their strengths and weaknesses. He is listening for any sign of leverage, for imbalances of power, and he is listening to understand what *they* want from the deal. Armed with this insight, the accomplished negotiator is in a position of strength before he even pulls up a chair at the negotiating table. In other words, he knows what his opponent wants as well as what brings him there, and the accomplished negotiator can expect to take away far more from the deal as a result. Knowing your opponent can make the difference between success and failure.

Perhaps no other skill can have such an immediate and measurable impact on a business. And there is surely no other central business skill that is practised and mal-practised so widely. Most of us negotiate, one way or another, almost every day, without realizing it. You don't have to be a top CEO or a hostage negotiator at the CIA to be interested in a subject we all have a stake in, even if we're not always aware of it. For we are all, by our very nature, negotiators.

Negotiation is hard work, and every act of negotiation takes a big personal commitment. Ultimately you are working to enter a contractual agreement, so in many ways negotiation is just the first phase in a much bigger process. You will have to live with the consequences of the deal long after the ink has dried on the contract, so be sure of what you want before you set out. And be sure, too, of what you don't want. You are under no obligation to continue with the deal if it turns out to be something that's not right for you. A lot of negotiation should be seen as a learning curve: identifying the possibility, or desirability even, of a particular deal, and then finding the people who could make it happen. The inquisitive negotiator then starts learning about his opponent, too. No two deals are alike, and every negotiation will take you on a very different journey from the one before – even if the client, the setting and the contract are to all intents and purposes the same.

Negotiation is, then, a big and broad and important subject, and is central to many situations in our everyday lives – as any parent rearing young children will tell you. In business, it is the great unseen and often unsung skill. It's at the heart of every strategy, every deal and every business relationship. It underpins every business plan, every sales target, every profit and loss sheet, every board meeting. We negotiate our way through our careers, and to a great extent through our wider lives, too. We negotiate our marriages, and how to end them. We negotiate for the houses we live in, and the loans with which to buy them. All the while, in the larger scheme of things, the wider world is kept safe by the various negotiated peace treaties, security agreements and checks and balances that maintain a broadly stable status quo. Negotiation is unquestionably a force for good, at all levels at which it operates.

To be consistent (and clear as to which party I am taking about), I refer to you, the reader, as the negotiator and the other party as the opponent. (They could, of course, be your employer, a client or business partner or occupy any number of other positions.)

In order to keep within a manageable scope, this book will primarily focus on how to negotiate for business. From to time to time, I will draw on examples from other spheres such as international relations, politics and even personal relationships. Yet it is the demands of the relationships that occur within the world of business that speak most acutely to the act of negotiating effectively (as well as being the main reason most of you decided to pick up this book).

Origins

Fittingly, the root of the noun *negotiation* is taken from the Latin *nego otsia* ('no leisure'). A lack of leisure sums up rather well how most citizens lived in ancient Rome – only the aristocracy found time enough to indulge in other pursuits. For centuries in Europe the verb *to negotiate* referred, literally and specifically, to doing business (French adopted *le négoce*). If you entered into negotiation in, say, sixteenth-century Paris, you were simply 'doing business'.

Only during the seventeenth century did the concept of 'negotiation' take on the modern-day meaning of a (normally face-to-face) dialogue between two or more parties with, generally, the aim of a mutually beneficial outcome.

One of the earliest examples of an international act of negotiation was the signing of the Franco-American Treaty in 1778. The treaty, negotiated by Arthur Lee and Silas Deane for the American side and by Charles Grevier and Conrad Alexandre de Rayneval on the French, established military protection for either country, should it be required (uppermost in French minds was an imminent invasion by the British). The 1778 treaty, which held until 1800, is remarkable as one of the first internationally negotiated military agreements. At the time, it broke new ground as the world's first trans-Atlantic treaty.

Since then, there have of course been many such international feats of negotiation, and the unprecedented upheaval – and violence – of the twentieth century proved fertile ground for negotiators as they strove to find common ground and set the foundations for what they hoped would be a safer, more peaceful world. An early peace treaty was the Treaty of Trianon in 1920, which set out the borders of an independent Hungarian state and marked a formal end to the horrors of the First World War. The Potsdam Agreement in 1945 was followed by the wider Paris Peace Treaties of 1947, which set a precedent for the sheer number of signatories to its accord.

The Cuban Missile Crisis of 1962 saw America's John

F. Kennedy sit down with the United Nations' Secretary-General, U Thant, and the Russians in a desperate and nerve-jangling effort to pull the world's trajectory back from the very brink of nuclear catastrophe.

Some historians see a further pivotal change in the evolution of negotiation immediately after the Second World War, when negotiation as a term applied to the more business-like, transactional form of discussions we are familiar with today.

Cultures

Over time, then, negotiation has evolved into the form we recognize today: a formal exchange along a general line of progress to finally agreeing some form of deal. But how this is done varies markedly across countries and cultures. North American negotiations are, by and large, a direct affair by international standards, working fast to establish consensus and resolve disagreements. This often leads to one side or both making concessions ahead of time, sometimes prematurely. Americans famously lay their cards on the table almost as an opening gambit.

Setting one's cards on the table is often seen as a last resort by the British, who prefer to use understatement and, in many cases, humour, to obfuscate and charm. Ultimately this can be very successful, but it's a method that's prone to inefficiency, and tends not to travel well. It can also leave foreign counterparts flummoxed.

The French will often subject their interlocutor to lively and often philosophical debate on each separate point, which can take some time. The Dutch, too, are prone to over-debate and often exhibit an almost paralysing obsession for analysis. And, while German negotiators place their emphasis on a rigid agenda and amassing their evidence beforehand, theirs can be a ruthlessly logic-driven approach, and highly effective. Perhaps it's because Germans take time to do their research, and will expect the same of you. They also expect you to be on time.

Arabs place a greater emphasis on getting to know their opponent, so expect to talk at considerable length about your life and family (and ask after theirs) before, gently, setting down to the matters of business. Negotiating in Iran can be circuitous and at times emotional, even passionate. In Singapore, fast and efficient is the norm.

Uppermost in many people's minds when thinking of international negotiation are the Chinese. As any foreigner who has undertaken negotiation in China will tell you, the experience can be a humbling one (and not a little exasperating). The Chinese could well be the world's master negotiators and, whether they are or not, certainly seem to believe it. There is one particularly important facet that differentiates Chinese negotiations from those with other nationalities. In China, the negotiation meeting itself is explicitly held in order to glean information on the opponent and the deal proposed. The discourse is often sharply, sometimes disconcertingly, direct. But the actual decision will often be made at a later date, sometimes with no further interaction with the other party, save to formally notify them that, should their deal go ahead, the following conditions must apply. Take it or leave it. The foreigner who looks east with a gleam in his eye would probably do well to secure a Hong Kong-based intermediary or moderator.

That other Asian giant, India, is much more gentle by

comparison. A languid, philosophical meandering will lead, eventually, to a set of deal-making tenets. But expect some playful ambiguity along the way. For if the Chinese are masters of negotiation (even if only in terms of their ruthlessness), Indians are the world's natural-born bargaining champions. Everything, but everything in India is negotiable, and is energetically and enthusiastically negotiated all day every day. Everything from rickshaw fares to restaurant bills and even wedding dowries. Almost every financial transaction on Indian soil is ripe for haggling.

Diplomacy

We've already established that negotiation is all around us, from the playroom to the boardroom. Uppermost in many people's minds when they think of negotiation is diplomacy, 'the art of letting someone else have your way', as David Frost memorably put it. Our time is replete with examples of diplomatic negotiations of epic proportions and almost without precedent. Britain is negotiating to leave the European Union. President Donald Trump is, as I write, in Singapore, negotiating for a denuclearized North Korea. And the European Union is re-negotiating with Iran to salvage what it can of its own nuclear deal, recently torn up by the United States. And many countries, from China to Canada, are looking to renegotiate their terms of trade with other countries on the back of recent tariffs imposed by the Trump administration. Now very much in the background to these, but no less complex given the number of opposing sides, are the on-off negotiations to try to bring an end to Syria's seven miserable years of civil war. These high-level, international, multi-party, high-stakes talks are some of the most complex and fascinating negotiations we will witness in our lifetimes.

Take the first of these, the so-called Brexit negotiations. A friend of mine summed it up rather well by comparing the process to one man (Britain) divorcing his 27 (EU member) wives all at once. Each wants to get the most from the deal, and they are generally not interested in finding win-win solutions. Indeed, the main reason the UK's negotiations to leave the EU are so protracted is precisely because the country's hand is weak. There are relatively few levers of influence it can pull – and a great many it is subjected to. Leverage from Brussels over the question of trade across what will become the country's only land border with the EU, the boundary between Northern Ireland and the Irish Republic, is evidence of this. Westminster views freedom of goods and people across the border, with an invisible EU/UK border dividing the Irish Sea, as 'unacceptable'. Yet Brussels argues that anything other than freedom of movement across the land border will result in the hard, checkpoint-lined border of the bad old days – something nobody wants to see a return to.

Behind these epic instances of international diplomacy are to be found heroes of negotiation, widely admired for their skill and dogged perseverance, often against all odds. John Kerry assiduously led negotiations with America's sworn enemy in Tehran, ultimately to triumph in 2015 with a deal that, 'without a single bullet being fire' (Barack Obama), saw the denuclearization of Iran in return for the gradual lifting of international sanctions. While the deal is now gravely threatened by the current White House administration, this should not distract from the monumental achievement of then Secretary of State John Kerry and his team under Barack Obama.

In August 2012 the then Secretary-General of the United Nations, Kofi Annan, suddenly tendered his resignation as the UN and Arab League special peace envoy to the nascent yet bloody conflict in Syria.

Annan had negotiated a proposal that called for the Syrian government to withdraw weapons and troops from strategic towns and cities across the already battered country and for rebel fighters to lay down their arms also. Annan's proposal set out a process for a wider transition of power that would ultimately lead to President Assad being replaced. Assad agreed to Annan's proposals, but his government chose to ignore the deal, and no rebel units disarmed.

Annan's position was fundamentally weakened by the fact that foreign signatories were divided on the course of action, and both Russia and China refused to sign an agreement that backed regime change. His fall illustrates the perils of multi-party negotiations, where many competing agendas often vie for dominance.

Observers blamed insufficient preparation before the agreement was drafted, which left some members of the Security Council inadequately briefed on the situation. Without a proper mandate, the deal fell through and one of the world's chief negotiators was left exposed and with little choice but to resign.

Nelson Mandela is another giant of negotiation of recent times. During his 27 years in prison, he negotiated with the African National Congress, then South Africa's pro-apartheid government. He spoke frequently with his adversary, F.W. de Klerk, over many years, and the two men forged a famously intense relationship over the course of their secret negotiations. Mandela's towering negotiating power, even from his prison cell, from where 'a victory over the white government was a distant if not impossible dream', spoke to the vital importance of talking, and continuing to talk. Nothing less than the end of South Africa's apartheid agony was, in effect, brought about by years of talking – by a prisoner serving a life sentence.

Types of negotiation

It's perhaps worth at this early juncture clarifying some terminology.

To *haggle* is to bargain or dispute the cost of a particular item. *Bartering*, while potentially ripe for negotiation, refers to an exchange of, say one commodity for another. In business, a barter agreement could involve a hotel advertising its rooms in a magazine and in return the magazine's directors get a certain number of nights in the hotel's chain worldwide. No money changes hands, but both sides benefit.

Today, there are two main types of negotiation widely recognized in the fields of business and international affairs. These are widely known as distributive and integrative negotiation, and while there are elements of both present in almost any form of negotiation, it is integrative negotiation that dominates most transactions and deals, discourse and diplomacy.

Distributive negotiation: this is the hard-bargaining, zero-sum brand of negotiation that opens with both sides adopting relatively extreme positions from which they seek to yield as little as possible. It is rarely adopted in business and, when used, seldom repeated. Its central belief is of a fixed value, a 'fixed pie', the existence of which makes the process more competitive. An example could be a customer looking to buy a Persian carpet. The seller sets the price at $1,000, but will try to find the minimum discount for the sale to go through. He might, say, offer $850 by gauging the buyer's 'walk-away' threshold. By ascertaining either side's walk-away value, each side will negotiate to minimize any deviation from their ideal price.

Distributive negotiation is the more entrenched, inflexible, form of bargaining. An example of distributive bargaining is President Trump's aggressive style of top-down negotiation over trade deals: insisting to Beijing, for example, that all imports of Chinese steel and aluminium will be met with tariffs. Instead of finding a more mutually beneficial solution, Beijing is responding with its own tit-for-tat tariffs on thousands of American imports. Ultimately this sort of quid pro quo results in higher prices and less availability, to the detriment of all parties.

Integrative negotiation: integrative, or principled, negotiation seeks to expand value to mutual benefit, rather than seeing it as a fixed entity, as is the case with its distributive cousin. The process aims to result in a gain for each side, the so-called 'win-win' tactics that form the basis of most day-to-day business deals. There may well be some immovable 'distributive' aspects there in the background, but they are not allowed to dominate the outcome, or tone, of the deal. Integrative negotiation hinges on mutual trust, problem solving and beneficial outcomes.

Integrative, or principled, negotiation is itself a strategy that aims to move both parties from more polarized positions and towards mutual interests. It seeks to find ways to satisfy both parties' goals while maintaining strong relations. Neither side feels taken advantage of. Sometimes two parties need to find a solution to a complicated conflict. In such instances, distributive negotiation will yield the best results.

A classic illustration of integrative negotiation and how it differs its distributive equivalent pictures two teenagers and an orange. If there's only one orange in the bowl and both teenagers demand it simultaneously, a distributive bargain would generally involve each of them getting half of it. In an integrative approach, each might ask the other why he wanted the orange, discovering in the process that one wanted to eat the segments while the other wanted the peel to bake a cake. The integrative bargain, if it works out this way, is obviously better for both.

In reality, integrative negotiation often contains elements of distributive negotiation – for instance, research has shown that conceding prematurely allows less scope for exploring areas for mutually beneficial outcomes, with a likely result more akin to distributive negotiations.

Whatever the category, the aim is the same. The art of negotiation is the art of reaching a compromise. The skills, stages and strategies that are outlined in this book, while placed more often than not in a business or trade setting, are eminently transferrable to other areas of life. In order to negotiate effectively, we all need to know some basic touch points. 'You have to go out and learn to negotiate – it's not a natural skill,' says Eldonna Lewis-Fernandez, author of *Think Like a Negotiator*. 'It's like playing baseball; you have to do it to get good at it.'[2] And the realm of business negotiation is a good one in which to start, for negotiation *is* the art of the deal. If successful, it really does mean getting to Yes.

Negotiation is about knowing what you want, going after it and being mindful of the other person in the process. A popular acronym often cited when talking about negotiation is WIIFM, or What's In It For Me? But perhaps a better, certainly more intuitive, approach, by way of starting to understand integrative negotiation and how it works, is to ask, WIIFT, What's In It For Them? Remember that the whole point of negotiating is compromise; meeting somewhere towards the middle. This means that while looking out for yourself, you need at the same time to remain focused on an outcome that will be acceptable to both sides. Remember, when you stand to leave that boardroom, you should have forged strong and positive working relationships, and not allowed bridges to be burnt along the way. One way to avoid the latter is to understand power, and how it works in the process of negotiation. And the subject of power is where we begin.

1:

POWER AND PSYCHOLOGY

Only free men can negotiate. A prisoner cannot enter into contracts
– Nelson Mandela[3]

Negotiation is such a familiar part of our everyday lives we often fail to recognize it's even happening, let alone identify the power battles and psychological warfare it entails. You do not need to be a lawyer to see negotiation and its inherent power struggles all around you. As a child, were you ever told you were good at manipulating your siblings? You were already good at negotiating. Ever bought a new car and offered to pay partly in cash? You are tapping into the seller's psychology, and doubtless being rewarded in return. Offering to pay up front is a good rule of thumb. It's even possible to negotiate with yourself. Even figuring out how best to carve up a full day, or trying to justify leaving work early – both can be settled with negotiation techniques.

Daily life involves negotiation to such an extent that we're largely unaware of it. Certainly, few people stop to think about it at all, let alone as an all but essential life skill. In busy everyday lives, we seldom pause to reflect that negotiating is, in fact, a complex and strategic mind game between two competing, but mutually intertwined, goals.

For life is dominated by negotiation. It shapes our interactions with others in both mundane and momentous ways.

Indeed, so much of our daily lives revolve around this practice, and yet so few of us spend much time at all truly learning what it takes to become proficient in, let alone master of, this requisite skill. It's worth, first of all, reflecting instead on how negotiation plays a central role in our day-to-day interactions with people around us. 'I'll take the kids to school, if you could pick up some milk.' Deal done.

The point here is that both parties get something they want, usually with some element of compromise. At the very least, both sides feel like they are on the winning side. This is the ideal scenario in almost all integrative negotiation. You might not really want to go out and buy a bottle of milk when it's raining, but at least you didn't have to do the school run. By meeting half way, life muddles through and advances in small steps.

People sometimes see attempts at negotiation as efforts to manipulate, or influence, others around us. Yet this is to misrepresent the process of negotiation, whatever the given situation. All negotiations involve some elements of give and take. Without mutual gain, why should the other side bother turning up? To understand the process of negotiation, and how to manage it to good effect, you have to understand the psychology at work in all negotiation discourse, no matter the setting or subject.

The psychology of negotiation

Surprisingly, many negotiators settle for less – at times even an outright loss – if they think the other side is losing more. In negotiation, psychology shapes all. Perceptions can lead to a palpable sense of power where none exists, and can leave participants feeling triumphant when, in reality, they lost. How can this be?

A fascinating paradox lurks at the heart of negotiation. It's empathy. Empathy is what enables both sides to meet half way; it's the force behind consensus. It's the enabler of those crucial concessions on the way to getting something, if not all, of what you set out to achieve. *Psychology Today* defines empathy as, 'the experience of understanding another person's thoughts, feelings, and condition from their point of view, rather than from your own. You try to imagine yourself in their place in order to understand what they are feeling or experiencing.'[4]

In negotiation, empathy is to understand the other's thoughts and, to some extent, their feelings. Being able to exhibit empathy is an absolute prerequisite for being successful at negotiation to any degree at all. Indeed, showing a lack of empathy can lead to all sorts of trouble, including acrimony, stalemate and ultimately the end of the relationship altogether. Empathy is so important because it's concerned with trust and integrity. Sympathy, with which it is often muddled, is how you feel as a result of another's situation. It is not necessarily to understand, and certainly not from their perspective. So empathy is crucial precisely because it's a two-way phenomenon. Like the wider bargaining within negotiation, it's a give-and-take exchange that is (or should be) integral to our approach. If this reciprocity is broken, offence may be taken and the results can be unpleasant.

Empathy is a paradox because while it's the elixir for mutual understanding, harbour too much of it and it acts a sedative that clouds judgement and leads to unnecessarily steep concessions being agreed to. Often painful concessions are borne purely by one party. Such as is the power of psychology. Be careful not to succumb to your opponent's charm: charm can be best described as 'empathy plus'. Perhaps this is why charm is often viewed with suspicion: an overly charming person can come across as less than trustworthy, as lacking in integrity.

Power, real and perceived

According to Google, *power* (noun) is defined as:

1. The ability or capacity to do something or act in a particular way

2. The capacity or ability to direct or influence the behaviour of others or the course of events

In the world of negotiation, the way in which power is exerted more closely, but not exclusively, fits with the second definition.

Power is the force that enables one party to gain from another in the course of negotiating. Notions of power are also interdependent, and interconnected. William Zartman asks: 'What are the interconnections among the various concepts of power – power as determined by the resources one controls, the relationships one has, the perceptions one holds. And what are the effects of power variously conceived on negotiated outcomes?'[5]

Power, and the balance of it, is crucial to understand if you are to find success as a negotiator. It's also the main reason many of us shirk from negotiating, or neglect to properly prepare, in the first place. Imbalances of power,

both real and per...
and are psychologi...
the weaker party to w...
er party, especially as...
side will stay on top. Tra...
tiation favours the notio...
negotiating 'ideal' from wh...
able outcomes are likely. Th...
is necessarily a path to some...
also a process that tends to red...
for the Lilliputian to enmesh the...
of him, is always there.

Remember, above all, that po... ...al or perceived. Which means that, taking int... ...ount actual power
imbalances between the parties, you're as powerful as your
opponent considers you to be. Use your power too force-
fully, and you will alienate your counterpart. Too lightly,
and you will risk appearing weak. Apply it to the wrong
variable, and you unhelpfully shift the course of the negotiations off the main agenda.

Power opens up possibilities within negotiations, ena-
bling holders to control the agenda, the course taken by
proceedings, and shapes the final outcome. In negotiation,
more than in almost any other realm of discourse, information *is* power. How you use this information depends on the
psychology at play.

Managing states of mind

In any agreement, it's important to consider how our minds
could be affected. When faced with a negotiation opportunity

...having the goal you want to ... , perhaps still somewhat abstract, ...any factors which inevitably influence ...egotiation and the perception of each of the ...ey information is exchanged.

...uch, the goal itself is not a fixed and immovable one, ...t is a marker that morphs and adjusts according to how the negotiations in hand develop. While this adaptation maintains an important flexibility throughout the process, just as importantly it provides a vital landmark – a bearing that anchors and reassures. Think of your goal as a lighthouse bordering a storm-swept sea, or a tree on the horizon that's swaying in the wind, but you're moving ever closer towards it.

A central part of managing states of mind is managing expectations, and these will themselves change depending on our mood – whether we feel at the moment a prevailing sense of success or failure.

With every concession, threat or delay, that original goal changes accordingly. Sometimes you may not even be aware of it, but your own perception will have changed from the original mission. In most cases, expectations become rather different (usually lower) than those we had formed at the outset.

So how to manage these expectations? Any concession from one side will generally raise expectations, and real prospects, for the other. If a concession is hard-won, expectations can raise considerably. In other words, even small concessions can be perceived as a success.

Likewise, a refusal will also mean a change in the expectations of the negotiating parties. By showing our opposition to the proposals of the other party in an assertive way, we will demonstrate that we are resolute in our conviction and, therefore, the expectations of the other party will change as a consequence.

Taking control

The side that manages to gain overall control gains a considerable advantage. A common way for people to attempt to assert their control is to draft the agenda. The topics to be discussed in the course of the meeting are then set out on your terms, covering your priorities. In this way, the agenda can be a tool to control the subsequent steps (see chapter 5).

The skilled negotiator will be wise to any advantage in setting out the agenda in a particular order. So where a negotiation or relationship is already strained, any controlling tactics should be applied very carefully; excessive or inappropriate control can easily break a potential partnership.

The immediate environment is another area in which control can be exerted. Hosting the negotiation in, say, your own boardroom is an obvious advantage. Your opponent will be on unfamiliar terrain, and may well be tired from travelling. The choice of location is undeniably very important. However, some negotiators find this 'home advantage' approach too blatant a tactic, and prefer to opt for a more neutral setting, such as a hotel business centre or lobby.

Hosting the negotiations also gives you the advantage of planning the seating arrangements. A more formal set up, with each side facing the other, is generally easier for both parties. An oval or round table can work well for smaller groups, but beware of mixing up the two sides: this can leave team members feeling isolated and awkward, especially if they do not know you well, or this is a first meeting.

As well as location and setting, time is another control factor. Very often, there is a lack of it. If your opponents are travelling, they may well have to adjust their plans if negotiations overrun. It's usually in both parties' interests to keep to the time allocated, and keep that to a minimum. Long-running negotiation is tiring for both sides, and can sharply increase the chances of conflict arising when low blood-sugar levels and fatigue kick in. In most cultures, it is polite to arrange for drinks and, if lengthier discussions are needed, light snacks. But be wary of heavier meals, as these are conducive to drowsiness and also to informality. Many businessmen make the mistake of allowing negotiations to continue over a lengthy, wine-fuelled lunch. In such instances, it is very common for both sides to concede to things they would not normally agree to, and the more laid-back, friendly ambience allows goals and clear perspectives to fade from view. Instead, better to invite your new partners to lunch once the deal is sealed and signed, and raise a glass to your mutual success.

Try to use time to your advantage: an efficient, shorter negotiation window can achieve better outcomes, with neither side feeling jaded and a healthy sense of momentum sustained throughout. We have all experienced the ennui of poorly managed meetings: negotiations are no different. Set a tight, workable timeframe that suits your agenda, and stick to it. The balance of power will work to your advantage.

Using information

Sun Tzu, the great Chinese military strategist and philosopher, says in *The Art of War* that every war is won or lost before it even begins. The same is arguably true of negotiation. Many people enter into negotiations having already made a fundamental mistake: focusing on the deal itself and not thinking about the process to get you there. In negotiation, information *is* power. And it is the act of taking the trouble to glean information beforehand that can decide the outcome of the negotiation to come. Perhaps the best advice to give anyone entering into a negotiation exchange is to be informed. Without information, you are entering blind, unaware of your opponent's background, business interests, their agenda and their motives. The more information you have before you start negotiating, the stronger your position will be at the outset.

Ideally, the kind of information you seek out is, within reason, the sort your opponent would rather you didn't have. But the power dynamics will already have shifted in your favour if you have obtained information the other side lacks, or is unaware of. Take time to do this (see chapter 3), even if this means delaying the day for the negotiation itself. Many things can go wrong along the way. And even a deal that seems strongly weighted in your favour can easily turn pear-shaped, hitting obstacles and getting caught up in conflict. In such situations, to be able to reach for that information you thoroughly briefed yourself with beforehand can save the deal.

Yet an extraordinarily high number of people fail to do this, and their experience of negotiation is often disastrous as a result. There is a clear importance to gathering and analysing information before and even during a negotiation. We are all prone to taking shortcuts, and many cannot be bothered to invest extra time gleaning relevant intelligence on the background of the deal in view. Our technology-driven era makes it simpler than ever before to carry out research. It is now possible to look up the company and its values, its ambitions and focus, all with a couple of clicks. Gathering the relevant information has always been an essential part of effective negotiation; undertaking this elementary research has never been easier than it is today.

Things to avoid

When thinking about the balance of power, it's important strive to avoid certain scenarios. Regardless of how the power dynamic seems like it's playing out, be careful to keep on a narrow path and not stray into territory that will aid your opponent, and risk lending them a more powerful advantage. Here, then, are some pitfalls to avoid, each of which can irrevocably shift power dynamics to the other party.

Their price: strive never to mention it. Talking about the other side's price or figure has the effect of immediately lending it credibility. In citing it, you endow it with a more public, shared, status. In the mind of your opponent, you have validated their goal, and the perceived power dynamics therefore shift in their favour. They see the momentum ebbing from your side of the table. Instead, use leverage to work to bring them closer to your bottom line.

To pre-empt being caught off guard, try to talk about the parameters in the early stages of your discussion. This makes it harder to be ambushed. With the boundaries established, you can progress with confidence, hopefully comfortable in the terrain that's been established. (Read more on strategy in chapter 4.) An effective alternative is to talk about range, rather than figures, and then work to move towards a number that is acceptable from both perspectives.

Acrimony: very simply, acrimony is a deal killer. Avoid it. And to avoid acrimony, avoid ambiguity. Ambiguity leads to issues being left unresolved, which is a central cause of acrimony. You need your opponent to feel on-side, and to be working with you towards that mutually advantageous outcome. Acrimony leaves people feeling sour and harbouring grudges. This is one of the biggest obstacles to successful negotiating. It is why divorce cases can take years to resolve, with both sides refusing to grant the other any concessions.

If hostility sets in, perhaps the best tactic is simply to pause, and look to resume talks at a later stage. Postponing negotiating allows both sides to cool off, gives time for reflection and helps any acrimonious feelings to dissipate. But extra time is also dangerous: the moment can pass, the idea can pale and your opponent could go elsewhere. Better still not to let acrimony enter in the first place.

Greed: setting your sights high is generally good. But aim too far and you can misfire badly. Negotiating for a salary raise? Careful: if you come across as greedy you could be fired – leaving you much worse off than when you started. As with prices, salary negotiations should have some boundaries established early on – ideally in the course of your research. Ask yourself, 'What can I reasonably get away with?' And go in from there.

The same principle applies in business deals: remember the other side needs to get something out of this, too. They don't want to feel hostage to your vision, or be bludgeoned into submission. Make sure you leave something for them on the table, too, and work to present this with persuasion and measured enthusiasm.

Emotion: showing almost any form of emotion during the negotiation process is essentially taboo. Displays of emotion, in almost any form, will make the other side feel uncomfortable. Emotion can rapidly lead to acrimony, and situations of conflict. This is because emotion contravenes two golden rules in negotiation:

1. Don't reveal too much

2. Don't take it personally

2:

ESSENTIAL SKILLS

A negotiator should observe everything. You must be part Sherlock Holmes, part Sigmund Freud
– Victor Kiam[6]

Never forget the power of silence, that massively disconcerting pause which goes on and on and may at last induce an opponent to babble and backtrack nervously
 – Lance Morrow[7]

Know what you want to achieve prior to starting to negotiate. It's the golden rule but the one most people fail to heed
– Ivanka Trump[8]

Learning to be an effective negotiator hinges on a set of core life skills, some of which at first appear to have only tentative connections to the parent skill of negotiation itself. In many ways this is why negotiation is a misunderstood skill – it draws on many different disciplines and schools, from acting to psychology, etiquette to strategy and strategic planning.

When setting out on a negotiation path, you need to be open to adaptive thinking across skill sets. Here, then, and set out over the following pages, are the top ten skills you need to be an effective negotiator. You need to learn to:

- **Observe**: be alert to your opponent, their behaviour, their language

- **Speak**: but only when appropriate

- **Question**: ask questions that are pertinent and timely

- **Listen**: take note of what you're being told and learn to use it

- **Use silence**: pause to prompt, disconcert and buy time to think

- **Make decisions**: forge decisions in the course of negotiation and keep to them

- **Prioritize**: keep those aims in view and in perspective

- **Apply assertiveness**: be firm without offending; use leverage to good effect

- **Solve problems**: recognize when problems are arising and know how to tackle them

- **Avoid emotion**: even in acutely stressful situations, learn to maintain diplomacy and a calm exchange

Observing

Be alert. Take note of your own language and behaviour as much as you watch theirs. Being observant in the course of negotiations extends to observing your opponent and also to being alert to your own motivations. You are, in effect, watching two parties at the same time: yourself and the other. You need to understand, first, what is motivating both of you and, secondly, be observing constantly the language, both verbal and physical, of your opponent.

Watch your opponent's body language in particular. Hand wringing is of course a sign of anxiety; so is holding onto the edge of the table. A lack of eye contact, and especially wandering eyes, can mean your opponent feels besieged, or in some way overwhelmed. Similarly, if they are frequently excusing themselves from the room, they could be feeling under pressure, and conferring backstage with a colleague.

Negotiation has been defined as a game wherein he who blinks first, wins. Eye contact is undoubtedly important. I have turned down job applicants who, in their interview, are unable or unwilling to make eye contact. Would they do the same to a would-be client? Probably. Making reasonable (not intense) eye contact reassures. It speaks to that elixir, empathy, we spoke of in the previous chapter. It helps to forge bonds of trust and marks the beginnings of familiarity.

If you strive to avoid making eye contact, your opponent would be justified in assuming you have something to hide. Even if, in reality, you are only grappling with shyness or feelings of insecurity, the lasting impression is one of disconnect. If you find making eye contact genuinely difficult (and many do), try looking at the bridge of your opponent's nose, instead. Either way, look directly at them, and tuck your chair to sit squarely opposite, with your head confidently raised, projecting an air of assured optimism.

Speaking

Practise speaking slowly and clearly. Keep sentences short. Use plenty of full stops. These provide rhythm and clarity, giving structure to your argument and lineage to your thoughts. Don't waffle, never mumble and avoid babbling. Waffling tells the listener that you've lost your way. It makes them think that you are not clear what they want – so why are they here? Mumbling is frustrating for the listener and can sound like you're obfuscating, reluctant to come to the point. Babbling, or talking too much and too quickly, signals nerves, a lack of proficiency and perhaps inexperience. Avoid all three. If you are in any way feeling uneasy about the upcoming conversation, ask a colleague on your team to help you in a role play. Enacting the negotiation beforehand and anticipating some of the questions and tensions in the boardroom by way of a dress rehearsal is often a very useful tactic, almost regardless of your level of experience.

Finally, be alert to your tone. Avoid 'upspeaking' – when you tend to lift up those words at the end of each sentence, so it sounds like a question? This might be acceptable in Australian soap operas, but try to avoid it when negotiating. Your tone should be calm and neutral. Upspeaking sounds friendly and informal, but lacks authority. Jim Camp, the author of *Start with No: The Negotiating Tools that the Pros Don't Want You to Know,* says using upspeak can make someone less likely to accept your request. 'It conveys that you're willing to move a lot if they don't like it,' he writes, 'When you make an offer on something, believe in it.'[9] In other words, match your tone to your situation. You're in a formal setting, at the apex of business activity. Strive to sound the part.

Questioning

Having just lambasted upspeak, I am now going to try to persuade you of the merit of asking lots of questions. Plenty of probing not only helps you to better understand your situation but also serves to impress, or even intimidate, your opponent. Questioning shows off two great qualities: that you're curious, and you're engaged.

Skilful questioning stems from an awareness that you can never know everything. Be alert to key information you may lack, and take the initiative and ask questions to fill in remaining gaps. Above all, questions encourage the other side to talk, which normally has the effect of making them like you more. It's a two-way street; you should expect some questions in return, and be ready for them. Questioning leads to stronger discussions, which are reassuring for both parties, and this in turn leads to more successful outcomes. Build specific questions into your planning and research.

Aside from gleaning information, smart questioning can yield a different sort of intelligence – for example, uncovering how technically sound your counterpart is on the topic under discussion. Or perhaps revealing how committed they are to their stated goals.

Questioning helps to determine how genuine the other party is, their levels of experience and even how likely they are to be honest in their dealings with you. An unproven conclusion is that women, while often more reluctant to negotiate than men, are often more effective owing to their readiness to question and empathize.

Particularly if something doesn't make sense to you, or the other side sends an email that comes across badly, never hesitate to pick up the phone. A huge amount can be resolved simply by talking directly about the task in hand, or the stage you're at. Don't let any hint of disagreement or ambiguity fester. It will only come back to haunt you, a bigger problem than before.

Listening

In order to negotiate, it's vital you learn how to listen. That may sound ridiculous, but a surprising number of people lack this ability. In negotiations, you need to listen in order to establish your next move. If you're not listening, that next move will probably look clumsy, ill-timed and out of place, and your opponent will seize on this as evidence you're not really up to the task. Assume the other side is using their language with care, that every word has a hidden intent, a specific purpose. With practice, and a disciplined ear, you really will start to hear your opponent's motives coming through in their language. Listening is an essential, basic skill in the art of negotiation as it enables you to figure out what motivates the other side. It will give you a distinct advantage so master it well – even if you talk less.

Using silence

When people stop talking, things start to happen. Just as nature abhors a vacuum, conversationalists tend to abhor silence. Most people, when conversing, do everything and anything they possibly can to prevent any pause from occurring. They stammer and stutter, change the subject, risk repeating themselves: anything to, if you like, silence the silence.

A skilled negotiator will use this inherent and widespread social dislike of silence to his advantage. Bill Coleman, the then CEO of Veritas Technologies, famously recounted that silence is '. . . a classic negotiation technique. It's a gentle, soft indication of your disapproval and a great way to keep negotiating. Count to ten. By then, the other person usually will start talking and may very well make a higher offer.'[10]

Silence can be a powerful tool for posing questions, setting their timing and adding to their impact. Use silence to frame your questions. Pausing before will give you more impact. A pause of three seconds before a question can emphasize its importance. If allowed, a three-second pause after a question should prompt the person on the receiving end to answer, rather than retort with a rhetorical question. By allowing a pause after their response you can sometimes encourage the other side to continue talking, revealing more detail.

There is a fine line to strike, though: timing is everything. Less than three seconds is deemed ineffective. Studies have shown that a pause of less than three seconds all but goes unnoticed. A three-second pause provides emphasis without being disconcerting. More than three seconds of silence is discomfiting, and this is another tool at the negotiator's disposal. At later stages, longer pauses can be justified, and indeed recommended.

Decision making

Decision making and problem solving are inextricably linked in negotiation. Decision making can be seen to be the more autonomous of the two, while problem solving almost always involves both parties, actively engaged with the issue at hand, and with each other's values.

The point here is that negotiation is a *joint* decision-making process, which involves both parties deciding which problems to solve and when. As with questioning, decision making is a skill that alerts us to any biases or weaknesses in the other side's arguments. Rational decision making hinges on both sides' reciprocity: identifying and solving problems along the way, to mutual benefit.

Much decision-making skill comes with experience. Over time, you learn to trust your own judgement, and that judgement, once proven, can become instinct. It's a mistake to stubbornly continue to back a misguided or erroneous decision. Many would rather continue down the wrong road than suffer the humiliation of changing their minds, but we all change our minds, more often than not on the back of new information. The really intelligent course of action is to admit this – just don't double-back too often, or you'll come across as indecisive and easily influenced.

Decision making is another skill that can be honed through enacting role plays with colleagues on your team.

Prioritizing

In order to prioritize, you need to know both what you want and how you intend to get there. Your main priority will usually be the business or opportunity offered by the prospect of the deal going through. There will simultaneously be several sub-priorities which the astute negotiator will juggle as he goes. Sub-priorities, which sometimes could be concessions, need to be decided while keeping the main objective in sight: keep your eyes on the prize, in other words. An example of a secondary priority could be a distribution agreement. But until you've signed the joint venture on the product itself, there will be nothing to distribute.

It's important not to get ensnared by lesser priorities that you have rightly identified, but that in reality risk becoming a distraction. So try to stay focused. You will generally achieve more if you prioritize less, i.e., you establish fewer goals.

Acting

A good actor can feign indifference, and this is exactly what you need to do in certain negotiations. It is a valuable but tricky skill to master. You are often very far from feeling indifferent, but it's imperative you don't let on. Adding to the pressure, a negotiator schooled in this art will himself be looking out for signs of acting in his opponent. Your performance needs to be polished, and this generally comes with practice. Some cultures imbue the negotiation process with a deep interest in the opponent's life and background. Under such scrutiny, feigning indifference for something that is not personal ought to be straightforward. Readers who have done any sort of business in the Middle East will know that business relationships can have an intensity not seen in other regions. As with all these skills, there is a balance. Do not act at the expense of your charisma. Everyone responds well to some sense of character. So be true to yourself, if not always to your motives. After all, this is business.

Controlling emotions

If you can meet with triumph and disaster
And treat those two imposters just the same
– Rudyard Kipling, 'If'[11]

It's common to feel both excited and anxious upon entering into formal negotiations. There is, after all, often a lot at stake. Negotiation can be an intimidating and stressful prospect. Knowing how to manage your emotions will make the process calmer, and more effective.

Emotion and negotiation do not mix well, and when the two combine unpredictability is the result, often with terrible results. The dynamics of negotiation are built on calm foundations. Brian Koslow advised, 'During a negotiation, it would be wise not to take anything personally. If you leave personalities out of it, you will be able to see opportunities more objectively.'[12]

Negotiation makes several demands of us. Chief among these is that we maintain self-discipline and are able to control our emotions. Of course, emotions and egos play a role in many deals – but they should not be allowed to dominate. Being hot-headed and appearing irrational will surely help no one. If you feel like leaving the negotiation, there is a way to do this (see chapter 8). But walking out should not be an aggressive or a snap decision in the heat of the moment. You will have almost certainly lost the deal.

In negotiation, at least for business purposes, we are concerned with the 'adult ego' (as opposed to the parent or child incarnations). The adult ego presupposes that we can recognize people and situations for what they are. We are, in other words, capable of objective analysis, able to resist being influenced by the emotional egos of parents and children.

Try to learn to manage, or master, any feelings of excitement and disappointment. They lead to your position being read too clearly, and advantage passing to the other side. At worst, they cause offence and lead to the negotiations being called off. At best, emotions can be harnessed, rather than suppressed, and used to drive the discussion forward. Think of it as adapting excitement into energy, or disappointment into resolve.

Remember, too, that if negotiation is the art of letting others have your way, it is also by necessity the art of accepting losses. There will be compromises, and these can be painful. Keep focused on the wider picture, and don't let your disappointments cloud either your judgement or your countenance.

Whatever you might be feeling, strive to be all but inscrutable in your responses. Even when the deal is done, and you came out on top, warmly congratulating the other party is both good manners and sound advice. The last thing you want is to come across as gloating, or overly content.

Similarly if a deal does not, for whatever reason, go your way, maintain a calm optimism that speaks to doing continued business in future. Very often they'll be back and next time it will be better.

Clarifying

It takes courage to step back and ask for clarification. No one wants to be thought of as slow on the uptake. But we have already seen how ambiguity breeds discontent, and the ability to recognize when to ask for more clarity is an important one. In communication generally, not just in negotiations, clarification means giving the recipient a clear and concise meaning. Asking for clarification reassures the speaker that he is being listened to, and that that listener is taking a real and engaged interest in what he is saying. More importantly, requesting – and providing – clarification gives both parties confidence that they understand the sometimes complex topics under discussion. Clarifying is, then, a skill for reducing misunderstanding, and is at the heart of all good communication practices.

Assertiveness

Assertiveness is not often thought of as a skill, but it is. It's the ability to apply pressure, or leverage, without the other side feeling suppressed or even being aware that pressure is being applied.

The first point to clarify is that assertion is not the same as aggression. Many mistakenly think assertiveness means being dominant and the pushing of your own set of requirements at the expense of others. An assertive person is open to and respectful of other people's views and positions. They communicate without causing offence. Assertion, used well, initiates actions and ideas, rather than reacting to something. It's a driver, a positive force in negotiation, and one that encourages mutual feelings of respect. Assertion helps establish authority, but it also breeds goodwill. Neither aggressive nor passive, assertiveness is perhaps the most overlooked skill in the negotiation toolbox. This could be because many people confuse it with negotiation itself. Rather, assertion is an aid to effective negotiation, and discourages overt displays of dominance. It is the skill that speaks most readily to compromise.

Be positive

Last but not least, train yourself to be positive. Learn to harness the power of positive thought. It sounds corny, but it's true. Positive thoughts have powerful consequences, so use them to your advantage. Research has found that entering negotiations with a positive attitude leads to higher levels of information exchange, stronger feelings of confidence and bonds of trust. Do not confuse a positive attitude with happiness, however. Happiness can be more dangerous. Happy negotiators are likely to concede too readily. Happiness is not an objective frame of mind, rather it is an emotion. Positivity is a frame of mind, and a positive attitude is infectious, makes those around you feel good and feel good about being with you, and lends the discussions momentum. A positive attitude fosters trust, facilitating the flow of information from one side to the other and back again, thereby helping to build a trajectory to success.

3:

KNOW YOUR OPPONENT

I will negotiate with my worst enemy
– Gavin Newsom[13]

From the classroom to the boardroom, free trade zones to war zones, negotiations are taking place all the time, the world over, as part of daily life. Successful negotiations hinge upon a clear understanding of your would-be opponent. But what approach should you adopt to achieve such a deep understanding in everyday business negotiations?

Whoever they are, your opponent is key to your success. That's why you're both there. Knowing who they are is crucial. You will go on to develop an intense relationship with them in the course of negotiating. You'll need to understand their motives, ambitions and values and use this information to establish boundaries and focus points, and anticipate their tactics. All this while maintaining excellent working relations and giving as little away of yourself and your company as possible.

Perspective taking

Who is this mysterious 'other'? The very way we refer to them is anti-consensus. The opponent, the other side, the third party – all these terms speak to division, a separation, and imply competition. It is true that both sides are in competition: competition for a sale, for carrying forward an idea, competing to be the firm or organization that wins the most advantageous/compelling/strategic/lucrative/prestigious deal. And each side will expect to come away with something worthwhile – or at least something that improves on their current lot.

There is, or ought to be, a burning desire to know about the other side. Try to establish who they are, and what makes them tick, early on. It will give you a tremendous advantage. Ami Gadhia, of Johns Hopkins University, put it rather well. She asked: 'What does the baseball World Series have in common with the [US] presidential debates? The participants have researched their opponents. Winning teams watch videos of their opponents' techniques. Political debate participants know each other's answers before they ask the questions.'[14]

Knowing more about your opponent enables you to understand, and even adopt, their perspective. Seeing things from their perspective involves understanding and anticipating their thoughts and behaviour.

An article in the April 2008 issue of *Psychological Science* explained how 'Perspective takers are able to step outside the constraints of their own immediate, biased frames of reference.' The authors of the article refer to research in which three studies were designed to assess the relationship between perspective taking and successful outcomes in negotiations:

> In two of the studies, the participants negotiated the sale of a gas station where a deal based solely on price was impossible: the seller's asking price was higher than

the buyer's limit. However, both parties' underlying interests were compatible, and so creative deals were possible. In the first study, those participants who scored highly on the perspective-taking portion of a personality inventory were more likely to successfully reach a deal.

In the second study involving the same gas station negotiation, participants were separated into three groups: the perspective-taking group who were told to imagine what the other person was thinking, the empathy group who were told to imagine what the other person was feeling, and a control group. The psychologists discovered that perspective-takers secured the most agreements and increased the satisfaction of their opponents compared to the control condition. Although empathizers produced the highest level of opponent satisfaction, they were less successful than perspective-takers at reaching a deal and thus failed to create long-term value for themselves and their opponent.

In the final study, participants were presented with a multi-issue negotiation regarding a job hire. Perspective-takers created more value and earned significantly more points for themselves than those from the empathy group or the control group. The empathy group, in contrast, obtained the fewest individual points.[15]

The results of these three separate studies imply that perspective taking is a useful trait to have, and that it makes a difference in negotiation outcomes. Perspective can afford particular insights that enable a deal to be structured that could benefit both sides. The studies above illustrate the dangers of too much empathy which, by contrast, can disproportionately benefit the other party. Remember, while rightly working to understand their perspective, not to lose sight of your own.

Research, research

In this technology-driven age, research is a doddle. Once you know what it is you'd like to find out, the rest is easy. Yet surprisingly few people bother to do it. A bit of investigative delving beforehand can put you at a superb advantage before negotiations even begin. You can know all you need to know before you've even met your opponents. Many of the horror stories you hear, when negotiations go bottom up and all is lost, stem from one side or both not doing their homework. This might sound implausible, but it's true. With Google never more than a finger-swipe away, there's no excuse for not embarking on some research. If this doesn't persuade you, then just imagine what they could be, and probably are, uncovering about *you*.

It should be stressed that this stage isn't (or shouldn't be) untoward or improper. You're not snooping, or prying. Researching is a logical step on the path to 'knowing your enemy', as it were. If the deal is worth pursuing, then set to work, comfortable in the knowledge that information is power.

So what information are you setting out to find?

Essentially you are seeking the answer to one question: Why us? What is it we have that they want? Carrying out preliminary research is one of the easiest parts of negotiation, and you should start with the obvious.

Check their LinkedIn profile and run a Google search on their company and its recent history. You should be able to bring up press releases and any filings with regulatory bodies like the SEC (in America), HMRC, the FCA or Companies House (in Britain). You're looking for evidence of previous deals: takeovers, mergers and acquisitions, new office openings – activities that indicate their ambition and reach. They could be registered in New York but run out of Singapore, with a new regional office in Hong Kong. Where are they headed next? Why are they interested in doing business with your firm? If this deal is successful, what is the scope for further opportunities down the line? In what ways do they differ from your organization? Compile a list.

What's the size of the company and how fast is it growing? Do they seem to be partnering with similar firms to yours? What sort of company is it? Career-oriented, networking sites like LinkedIn and Glassdoor can give an indication of high staff turnovers, and any management instability. Is the company publicly listed? If so, since when? How have the shares been faring? Publicly listed or privately held, who are the major shareholders? Who sits on the company board? And which of those members makes the important decisions? Who's the boss, and what is their reputation? What sort of personality are they? Even larger organizations can take their overall tone from the top. Regardless of who your contact is, find out about their CEO.

Is management one and the same as the company ownership structure? Probably not. Look into this. I was once offered a job running the publications for a 'London-headquartered' media company which, it turned out, housed the main offices in Istanbul. The business was run out of Dubai and was registered in the British Virgin Islands. 'London-headquartered' amounted to nothing more than a PO box posturing as a street address. Make of that what you will.

Try to find out any industry-relevant experience they have, and any significant gaps. Is this in fact a good match? Are they the right partners for this deal? Now's the time to find out. Are there other areas you could collaborate on also? Compile these, and any other, notes and you'll have a file that should prepare you well and give you added confidence when stepping into the boardroom.

Establishing boundaries

Before you get there, it's important to sustain contact with the other side as much as you deem is necessary. One reason for this is to define the boundaries of your prospective deal. The scope of the deal should be set out and clearly defined as early as possible. This exercise alone is very useful in quickly bringing to light any misunderstandings or areas that are irrelevant to the deal. Establishing boundaries is reassuring for all parties. Ensure both parties set out their goals, and clarify them, along with any caveats and measurements, before you begin negotiating for real.

Withholding information

As you research your opponent, you need to bear in mind that they could be deliberately withholding information from you. This is a reality of negotiation, and one you should be prepared for – as far as you can prepare for something you don't know, that is. Different studies have consistently shown that around half of all negotiations involve lies. Hence deception is one of the intangibles that negotiators must try to prepare for, and take reasonable measures to prevent. In this era of fake news, it should come as no surprise some people are prepared to lie in order to gain some advantage, perceived or real. You are likely to frequently encounter people withholding information, although you won't always be aware of it. The best insurance is, of course, to undertake your own research thoroughly, thereby limiting their scope for underhand tactics, or a cover-up.

Obviously if it turns out they are up to no good, or are being dishonest, you should walk away. But understand that in the vast majority of cases (even if 'lies' are told in almost 50 per cent of negotiations), your opponents are withholding strategic information for their own benefit, rather than actually trying to undermine you. Remember, too, that drip-feeding information (while holding some back) can improve the overall outcome. You shouldn't put all of your cards on the table at the outset.

McDonald's, the ubiquitous American hamburger chain, was rapidly expanding in China in the 2000s, and sent in a team in 2002 to buy up various strategic sites for new branches of its international franchise. The global fast-food giant, well versed in deal making around the world, did its homework and found that an inexpensive site, with approval for development, was for sale on the fringes of a burgeoning city near Nanjing. Moreover, McDonald's discovered the local government had approved the construction of a big housing development on the lot adjacent to its new restaurant. During negotiations, the restaurant did not let on that it knew about the residential project – or it would have invited the seller of the first lot to raise his price. The onus is, unfortunately for that Chinese farmer, on both parties to be fully briefed on the deal at hand – even if it means a trip to the local governor's office to view their list of planning applications.

Agendas and motivation

Research shows you are more likely to achieve better outcomes by ranking your goals in advance. That way both parties can compare their rankings and determine what the full set of options really are. This more transparent approach extends into the negotiation room later on, whereby all the issues are left on the table for discussion.

Being more upfront enables both sides to anticipate the other's tactics. And there is no harm in this. Time for planning earlier on helps to minimize risk of surprises at more crucial stages. Everyone will have their own agenda, with their own goals and targets. The more transparent you can be about these, the better. Talk your agenda through with the other side by way of reassuring them you are a suitable partner.

Managing expectations

Sharing your agenda, and being open about goals and targets, makes managing expectations much easier, as both sides already know a good deal about the other's motives. Successful negotiators strive to ensure both sides are content with the deal as it's set out in the preliminary stages. This is partly because they know that a satisfied counterpart is more likely to do business with them again in the future. You should work hard to ensure your opponent's expectations are fair, and in line with the deal as it is set out. Dealing with inflated or unrealistic expectations is a major cause of negotiations failing.

Research has shown that negotiators tend to instinctively compare the real outcome with the result they were anticipating before they started formal negotiations. As a result, two parties experiencing precisely the same result can in fact have very different responses to the deal.[16]

Consider, by way of example, two property buyers who both buy a similar apartment in the same street. Both apartments sell for around $800,000. The buyer who expected to pay $700,000 will be dissatisfied with this deal while his new neighbour, who was braced to pay upwards of $850,000 will be rather pleased. Perceptions are powerful influencers.

4:

STRATEGY

You do not get what you want. You get what you negotiate
– Harvey Mackay[17]

What is a strategy?

Strategy is, according to Google, one of two things:

1. A plan of action designed to achieve a long-term or overall aim

2. The art of planning and directing overall military operations and movements in a war or battle

For a single definition, strategy can be thought of as *a plan of action designed to achieve a particular goal.* This definition is central to our thinking on negotiation. If planning and preparation are the key to success in negotiations, then strategy is the key to sound and effective planning. The two are inextricably bound together. Strategy is the method supporting your motives, the master plan underpinning your aims. This chapter considers how to formulate good, effective strategy.

Though strategy is an important, even essential, consideration when approaching a negotiation, it is curiously overlooked. In my pile of books on and around the subject of negotiation, only one even mentions strategy in its index. How can this be? For strategy has, in recent years, become a buzzword in the world of business. Many companies, large and small, have entire departments dedicated to strategy. The head of strategy is to all intents and purposes more senior than the head of development: he is setting out the company's master plan – the road map to success. A firm's business strategy is a summary of how it intends to achieve its goals. The negotiator's strategy is exactly the same. Moreover, developing the ability to think strategically is an extremely valuable tool for negotiations.

Knowing what you want ought to be easy. Yet many people put themselves in important situations – asking for an increase in their salary, for example – without ascertaining beforehand what leverage they have and where their maximum sustainable position lies. Most vitally of all, many people worry they will appear greedy, or are anxious not to offend their opponent. Setting out a good strategy can help mitigate these feelings, clarifying as it does the path that lies ahead. It also encourages you to figure out the other side's interests.

What is standing in the way of mutual agreement? Are they aware of your underlying interests? And do you know what your underlying interests are? If you can identify their core interests as well as your own, you will be much more likely to find a solution that benefits both sides.

You must analyse the potential impact of the agreement you are advocating, as the other side would see it. This is essentially the process of assessing the deal's merits and weaknesses, but you should make an effort to do it from the other side's perspective. Carrying out an empathetic analysis such as this will help you understand where your opponent is coming from. You should find you are then in a better position to negotiate an agreement that will ultimately be acceptable to both of you.

Yet, to enter into negotiation is, as we've already seen, to beneficially take advantage of each other in some way. Without you fully asking for what you want (or more), your opponent is in a stronger position to take advantage of you. First and foremost, he will surely work to negotiate you down, so you have little to lose by starting high.

If your first offer is rejected out of hand, you can always make the other side a counter offer. Or should you invite them to go next, and tell you what is acceptable to them? This second tack is risky – it could reveal an all but unbridgeable gulf. But it is at the same time likely to wrong-foot your opponent. After all, remember they are only sitting at the table with you because they, too, want a deal, and a workable one.

It is strategy, and more specifically strategic thinking, that steers the parties through to success, working to preempt difficulties and obstacles along the way.

Strategic thinking

Strategic thinking defines the way in which people think about, assess, shape and ultimately create, the future. Strategic thinking relies upon mastering a series of critical and interrelated skills. The most effective strategic thinkers use them every day. The US-based Center for Strategic Planning[18] identifies a core set of eleven critical skills:

1. The ability to use both the left (logic) and the right (creative) side of the brain.

2. The ability to think with a strategic purpose while creating a vision of where they're going. They manage to blend the two skills, which feed into each other.

3. The ability to clearly define objectives, with tasks aligned to a specific timeline.

4. The ability to integrate their plans with flexibility by building in benchmarks which they adjust as plans are revised along the way.

5. They anticipate change and seek to challenge the status quo. In other words, they are proactive, not reactive.

6. Perception: they recognize often subtle clues to inform and guide their strategic direction. Good strategic thinkers and excellent listeners are alert to any new or relevant information that can guide them.

7. Lifelong learning: they are unceasingly inquisitive and curious.

8. They actively seek out advice from others.

9. A tremendous creativity is imbued with a sharp sense of realism – they are alert to what is achievable in the medium to longer term.

10. They are non-judgemental. They encourage ideas and brainstorming, and are careful to avoid unnecessary criticism.

11. They have a limitless capacity for patience, ever

mindful that ideas and strategies take time to develop into success.

Implementation

Strategic thinking often starts with a company's business plan. The plan articulates the mission and vision of the company and evaluates its management, products and market. Usually strategic planning proceeds by conducting an analysis of the key strengths, weaknesses, opportunities and threats a business might be facing – the popular SWOT analysis.

Smart negotiators embrace any weaknesses or threats that are revealed. Aided by their strategic thinking, they work to address them, or profit from them. For example, the strategic thinker might assess a saturated market, in which received wisdom says there is no room for a new arrival on the scene. The strategic planner will home in on any niche in that market and work it to his advantage in ensuing negotiations.

Aligning strategy with situation

Michael D. Watkins has written extensively on the importance of matching a strategy to a situation and ensuring that it is grounded in absolute reality. Professor Watkins encapsulated his theory in his STaRS model: Start-up, Turn-around, Realignment and Sustaining success. The model is often used by strategic planners ahead of negotiations to help them to figure out the background to the proposed deal, and where they could take it. Watkins sought to give reforming strategies in business a framework, which clearly identifies each stage.

A book on how to negotiate does not really need to look in detail at the four stages to the model, but rather to recognize the core message of Watkins' theory: the more fluent you become in reading the landscape around you, the more effective you will be at leveraging the system, exerting your influence and applying your effort in ways that maximize impact.

PayPal, the online payments system founded in 1998 by Elon Musk and four others, today posts annual revenues of more than $13bn. On the back of one of the most impressive business strategies in recent times, if not ever, at time of writing PayPal commands more than 20 per cent of all online payments made in America, and processes fully 62.7 per cent of online eWallet payments. The company makes enormous profits without actually making anything at all. And it did this by disrupting one of the hardest of all industries to disrupt – banking.

PayPal's founding quartet had a bold strategy and set about implementing it ruthlessly. Their first move was to partner with eBay to process the online retailer's payments directly. It dared to challenge the status quo, bypassing the banks altogether to partner directly with retailers – a strategy banks have always shunned in favour of payment-processing middlemen such as Visa and MasterCard. PayPal's daring strategy had a secondary, increasingly valuable, advantage: by working with retailers, PayPal garners vast amounts of data on what buyers are spending where. All that the banks see and know of the transaction is a single, terrifying, word: PayPal.

Types of negotiation for the strategy

The first thing the strategist must decide is which type of negotiation he is going to be working with. Over the course of this book, we are most concerned with integrative, or principled, negotiation, as set out in the introduction. To recap, integrative negotiation is interest based: it attempts to improve the likelihood of both parties achieving something of their stated goals by exploiting the fact that each side will value the outcomes differently.

Integrative negotiation differs from its cousin, distributive negotiation, which assumes a fixed value that is to be divided between the parties. In a distributive negotiation, each side often adopts an extreme or fixed position, knowing it will not be accepted and then seeks to cede as little as possible before reaching a deal. Distributive negotiation is sometimes referred to as 'hard-bargaining' negotiation, whereas integrative negotiation is seeking to enlarge the pie, aiming for a 'win-win' result, with both sides walking away happy.

We have already seen that integrative negotiations are built on mutual trust, and this is a key source of leverage for the skilled strategist. Integrative negotiations will, if successful, work to ensure that mutual respect and integrity are used to build a common problem-solving approach.

Tactics

The terms *tactic* and *strategy* are often confused and are sometimes wrongly used interchangeably. Yet they are quite distinct, and one constitutes the sum of the parts of the other. A tactic (from 'the art of arrangement' in ancient Greek) is an action aimed towards achieving a specific goal. The strategy is the umbrella above the set of tactics, pulling them together cohesively and in one direction. Strategy is the overarching campaign plan, but within and beneath it are tactics.

Tactics can help enforce power dynamics: they are used by those with the power, or the confidence, to apply pressure on their opponents. Tactics are so widespread that they often go unnoticed. Sometimes this is because they are applied so skilfully, but it's important to become adept at seeing them for what they are. Once you start tactic-spotting, you'll see that they are used everywhere – and in all walks of life.

Key tactics for successful negotiation strategies are:

- **Preparation**: the number one tactic is to be prepared. Take time to do that crucial research. Establish their competitors' pricings and offers.

- **Initiative**: be the one to draft the first version of any agreement. This tactic allows you to frame how the deal should be structured.

- **Goodwill:** keep the negotiations courteous and positive in tone. Establishing a good long-term relationship should be one of your top priorities in the negotiation.

- **Listen**, and refrain from talking too much.

- Understand the **dynamics** at play. Identify who has leverage and what their constraints might be in terms of time or scope. Be clear as to what advantages either side holds.

- Be prepared to **walk away** if the terms are not attractive and appear immovable. But back up your arguments with research beforehand. Know, for example, the market prices for what is under discussion.

- **Time**: manage it well. Time is the enemy of many deals. Your strategy should allow for efficient and effective negotiations. Seize on momentum, and remember the longer a deal takes to complete, the more likely it is to run into obstacles.

- If no contract is signed on the day, a good strategist promptly prepares a **letter of intent** to summarize and record the main points gleaned from the negotiations.

- Ask plenty of **questions**.

- Always **counter**. Never accept the first offer. Not countering can have serious consequences. In the absence of a counter offer, your opponent could well conclude that they gave away too much and attempt to escape the deal. Lay the groundwork to avoid instances of buyer's remorse.

Break-out sessions

Strategists often like break-out sessions. These can be planned or spontaneous, and allow for satellite groups, made up of either party, or the main negotiating team itself, to discuss specific topics, assess their progress or seek wider counsel or advice. As negotiations tend to be intense affairs, break-out sessions appeal to the consensual, positive nature of many strategists. The pause from formal negotiations can help defuse tensions, give both sides some off-the-record time to gather their thoughts and simply take a short break from proceedings before returning refreshed and re-briefed.

Salaries

A footnote to this chapter takes a look at one of the most popular forms of negotiation: asking for a pay rise. We have all found ourselves, at some point or another, in that rather awkward situation of asking for more.

'If you don't ask, you don't get' rings particularly true when it comes to negotiating pay. Negotiating a rise can make a big difference, and not just in the short term. Research has shown that female employees, who are for various reasons often more reluctant to ask for a rise, lose out over their career by as much as $1.5m, according to Linda Babcock[19] of Carnegie Mellon University, and co-author of *Why Women Don't Ask*. Babcock conducted a study of 78 master's graduates, and found that only 12.5 per cent of women negotiated their starting salary compared to 52 per cent of men.

Salaries and fees can be tricky things to negotiate. And yet the same rules tend to apply as for wider negotiations. As with other forms of negotiation, it's normally good practice to make the first move on your price, but as Chris Voss, author of *Never Split the Difference*, recalls in an instance from 1940s Hollywood, this approach can be hazardous, unless you are well informed:

When the famous film writer Billy Wilder went to hire the famous detective novelist Raymond Chandler to write the 1944 classic *Double Indemnity*, Chandler was new to Hollywood. But he came ready to negotiate, and in his meeting with Wilder and the movie's producer, Chandler made the first salary offer: he bluffly demanded $150 per week and warned Wilder that it might take him three weeks to finish the project.

Wilder and the producer could barely stop from laughing, because they had been planning to pay Chandler $750 per week and they know that movie scripts took months to write. Luckily for Chandler, Wilder and the producer valued their relationship with Chandler more than a few hundred dollars, so they took pity on him and called an agent to represent Chandler in the negotiations.[20]

One reason it's best to go first is that your employer is going to be more concerned about his costs and bottom line than your ability to pay the rent each month. So he may well offer you something that, in reality, you will barely notice month by month. With the right arguments, and sufficient leverage applied with tact, you can change, say, a 3 per cent rise to a 23 per cent or even higher.

If you are planning to go first, set your figure in context. Cite salaries at rival firms for roles at similar levels of seniority to yours. This can prompt your boss to think more from a defensive position and shift the discussion onto a 'bolstering range'. Columbia Business School has published research by psychologists that shows that people who offered a realistic range, the so-called 'bolstering range', rather than a specific figure, tended to receive significantly higher salaries than those who specified a number.[21] The bolstering range is framed by the absolute top value you think you could achieve, and the lowest figure you could reasonably accept.

With rise requests, it's particularly important not to jeopardize any goodwill by making your request sound like an ultimatum. Basing it on market forces is one point of leverage, as is good performance – albeit aligned to the passage of time. Keep a record of your accomplishments and achievements, and report regularly to your manager. Build up a strong dossier of 'evidence' to support your eventual rise. But when the time is right, do not hesitate. You are always going to be your own best ambassador – few others will champion your cause. A good boss will understand this, and appreciate your candidness.

Sometimes you can make the request more acceptable by, say, asking for a slightly smaller rise in return for some remote working each week. Or more flexible working hours. These kinds of practices are becoming commonplace, so if money is not the sole factor from your side, consider offering some extras to make the deal go through.

In short, make an honest, well researched and timely case, and set out a 'bolstering range' that at least overlaps with what you expect you could achieve. Keep it realistic, and above all avoid an ultimatum – or you might find you've been fired instead.

5:

KEY STAGES

Prepare to win anywhere in the world
– slogan for Harvard Law School's programme
on negotiation

*A good plan is like a road map: it shows the final
destination and usually the best way to get there*
– H. Stanley Judd[22]

Think of negotiation as a process towards a specific outcome. That process is often imagined within the setting of
deal-making : the orb of a single lightbulb in an otherwise
dark room, late at night. The poker-faced inscrutability of
the 'players' as the opponents grind each other down into
the small hours. In reality, a lot happens before entering
that dimly lit chamber of popular imagination. Whatever
the stage and set, the players need to rehearse. There are
plots to uncover, lines to learn and scenes to be acted out in
sequence before the opening night.

The planning stages often get overlooked because it's off
set and lacks the glamour and excitement of the real thing.
Yet, followed through, these simple steps arm you with the
knowledge and confidence you need to come out with what
you want to achieve.

Some people add more, categorize differently or pro-
pose different labels, but the process is at its heart essentially

the same, and can most succinctly and simply be described as involving five broad steps that help lead towards a successful outcome. The key stages together equip you with the road map to where you're going. They are:

1. Preparation and planning

2. Defining the rules

3. Clarification and problem solving

4. Bargaining

5. Closure and implementation

If you're new to negotiation, or lacking in experience, make a point of following these stages carefully. Adhering to them, and building them into a workable agenda with sufficient time for each stage will hugely increase the chances of a successful outcome.

Some stages will take longer than others. And every negotiation is different. Yet the process is largely the same. Imagine you're in deep in the warrens of the Grand Bazaar in Istanbul and you're looking to buy a carpet. Following the above stages, you'll broadly:

1. Prepare by sussing out what others have paid for similar carpets (taking into account size, provenance, condition).

2. Rules can be trickier in a real marketplace, but the first and most crucial is: let the seller go first. So prepare by figuring out how you're going to withhold information, knowing you'll probably come under pressure to disclose it.

3. Clarify key factors, such as competition. Are there other carpet sellers nearby? (Plenty.) Are they offering similar value? (Probably.) If competition is high, this will put you, the buyer, in a stronger position. But if you are just one of hundreds of Western tourists, that could weaken your hand. Try to gauge how much business they are trading.

4. When preparing to bargain, know what you would like to pay – or what you can afford. Set your desired price, and establish this in your mind as your goal. When it comes to numbers, try to get them to go first (they will do the same with you; it can be an endurance test).

5. Over (very) sweet *çay*, the Turkish carpet seller will try to 'sweeten' you out of driving a hard bargain. Remember this is a game, and the back-and-forth nature of the bargaining is expected. Both sides by now have come some way from their opening extremes. But you're not yet at your target price: your pocket's budget. Having haggled away that cushion you built in (the bolstering range) politely thank the seller, and go to walk away. Success? There's a fair chance.

Negotiating in a foreign country, particularly in the lively and often bewildering setting of a bazaar, is never easy, but it should be fun. But whatever the setting, the course of any negotiation can never be entirely predicted. However, following these five steps can go a long way to minimizing uncertainty. If these stages are not built in, and taken into account, your control over the agenda risks being lost, or getting bogged down by the other side's priorities. Following the key stages, with any annotations and subjects for discussion integrated, will nudge you along the path: a road map you can keep returning to at intervals, reorienting if necessary before continuing towards your destination.

Stage one: preparation and planning

Preparation and planning is the first step in any negotiation process. It is undertaken in advance of formal negotiations, and is arguably the key to success, as we've already touched upon. (See chapter 2, for the importance of research in preparing for negotiations.)

Preparation is one of the most important elements to get right because without a plan you have no guidance from which to take control. Very often it is only with hindsight that its role in clinching the deal is properly revealed. If you are disciplined, and prepare and plan in advance, you will start to see the results of your efforts and foresight. Preparation creates value.

In the course of your preparations, remember that every negotiation you take part in will be unique. No two are alike. Even in a new negotiation between the same parties for the same product or service, the dynamics will shift, markets wax and wane, your relationship itself will on a different keel each time – as will the timings. Try, then, to pre-empt this inevitable unpredictability in your planning.

Many people instinctively think of planning as a solitary stage, but in fact it's far more effective – and enjoyable – to prepare as a team. First, it helps to strengthen the idea of that you really are a team, on the same side. And second, it ensures everyone has the same exposure as ideas are generated and strategies put in place. Working as a team helps to ensure you are all thinking along the same lines – and helps to minimize the chances that one of you will stray from the party line on the big day. Even if you are a team of one, invite a close colleague to help you – offering a valuable second opinion, for example, or running through the various scenarios for the pitching, in the form of a role play.

Remember, also, that the preparation stage is your opportunity to establish your aims but also your variables (see below). Try to discuss these with your opponents at an early stage, certainly before the negotiations themselves. This is very important if you're to avoid unwanted surprises further down the line. There are generally five variables under discussion in most forms of business or trade negotiations. These are:

- Pricing: referring to a fee, the price or the value of the deal

- Volume/scale: how much

- Delivery: when and where

- Contract: when it starts, and when it ends

- Payment: terms, currency and method

There can be other variables, depending on the type of deal. Some might be concerned with geography or particular territories; others might specify a particular purpose, such as a distribution agreement, or an advertising campaign.

Allow time, with your opponent, to properly understand the list of variables and what their criteria are. Variables are at the heart of the preparation and planning stage: building any value in negotiation generally involves trading lower-cost or smaller-volume/scale variables for higher-cost or larger-volume/scale. The added transparency both sides will have gained from discussing the variables beforehand will enormously improve both sides' chances of a successful deal. It's worth looking at each in some detail:

Pricing: the price of the deal can be affected by many factors, of course, but there are some particular issues that should be taken into account. How is the product or service to be used? Is it part of a big, thriving and competitive market place? Or is it a niche, bespoke product sought after by those who need it?

Consider also such factors as geography: to which regions does the deal apply? Who will be benefitting there? And how important is the client to this deal? What sort of relationship do you have, and what is their loyalty?

Volume/scale: economies of scale are universal. In almost all deals there is a direct correlation between volume, or scale, and price. Even with a single product or campaign, the deal will more than likely be shaped by the reach (or scale) of distribution, or the size of the market.

Some companies publish price lists that clearly build in discounts linked to volume purchases. Such tariffs can help to stave off further negotiations on the price, but this cannot be guaranteed.

Delivery: when is the contract launched? It could be signed today for delivery tomorrow, next week or even next year. Whenever the stipulated delivery date, factor in consequences for late delivery. Not meeting delivery commitments should be taken seriously, and the risk of this happening needs to be factored into the contract. Once signed and agreed, delivery should cease to be a variable quantity.

Sometimes the other side will claim circumstances beyond their control, such as extreme weather conditions affecting shipping. Try to ensure there's a clause in the contract that addresses this, specifying a delivery schedule and which party is responsible, by when. This could stipulate a penalty, a reduced fee or an 'sweetener' being given by way of compensation, such as free warehousing.

I used to run a book publishing house. Most of the titles related to the Middle East, but we would print them in China. On one occasion, the first batch was misprinted, which meant they had to be reprinted and risked missing the launch in London. We negotiated that one box of advance copies be air-freighted, and the remainder of the consignment be shipped free of charge at a later date. We benefitted from having the shipment fees waived, and the printer was able to remedy a less-than-ideal situation by printing the bulk of the order in a later, more off-peak, slot.

Contract: setting the duration of the contract is a particularly important consideration. Get it wrong, and the deal is worthless. Time, or more specifically, *timing*, can be a very powerful tool in negotiation. Time and circumstance affect the value of almost everything in business. The same service or product delivered in a different time slot can make an enormous difference to the worth of the deal. For example: a product is launching in October, and a deal is under discussion for an advertising campaign to support its release. But, due to poor forward planning, there are no advertising slots available until October itself. In this scenario, the deal is greatly diminished, if not a write-off. A savvier negotiator would build in a three-month window for campaign running from August and leading up to the launch in October. Suddenly the deal looks like an attractive proposition, in a workable timeframe, and is worth a lot more as a result.

An awareness of your opponent's time pressures is, then, an important consideration when at the planning stage. Knowledge of their schedules can provide you with some powerful leverage.

Linked to timing are deadlines. Deadlines can help to exert pressure, yet the worst deadlines in negotiation are sprung at the last minute, when you're trying to close the deal. Deadlines can be real or artificial. One party could claim their offer expires after a certain time. Make sure these considerations are accounted for in your planning, to minimize the risk of being caught out.

Payment terms: the most important part of the contract when it comes to minimizing risk. Payment terms are normally reflective of the service/work/product's timely delivery. It's often a good idea to schedule in staged payments. A standard contract might set out: payment to be made in three equal sums, one, upon signature of contract; two, upon client approval of the finished project; three, upon receipt of finished goods.

Some contracts come with sharper teeth in the form of penalties for late delivery (or even late payments).

Stage two: defining the rules

You're almost ready to begin negotiations. But before you do, you need to try to bring order to a potentially chaotic, and certainly unpredictable, scenario. Two parties meeting with different aims and different ideas about how to obtain them can make for colourful encounters. You must strive to avoid this. Instead, having done your planning, put in place some rules – boundaries, if you will – to remind both parties of the agreed limitations to this deal. The rules set out the scope, but also the mode in which you'll be working. A set of guidelines could specify who sets the agenda, how long it is, which topics are to be discussed and in what order, and what the stated outcome will be. The rules can also specify where the negotiation will take place, and the allocated timeframe. Will there be one session or several? Remember time kills deals, so try to limit this. But in reality, many negotiations do need a second or even third session before finalizing. It depends on their complexity, and sometimes on the number of parties involved. The more people involved, the more is at stake, and the more strained the integrated negotiation model will become.

Stage three: clarification and problem solving

Remember that the point of negotiating isn't just to find an agreement, but a workable one. Be sure in advance the deal you are seeking can be implemented, then work to make sure it happens. Be careful of the other side claiming victory prematurely. A measure of success is not, say, the kidnapper exclaiming 'It's a deal!' – rather, the deal being finalized is signalled by the hostage walking free. Maintain perspective, and be clear from the outset as to what you're trying to achieve.

By involving both parties in preliminary planning and discussions, many would-be problems and snags can be ironed out before negotiations properly begin, and resolving them becomes more difficult. Set out where you're planning to go with the negotiation, ideally in a frank conversation with your opponent. Discussing the process is a great way to clear up any misunderstandings, pre-empt conflict and reassure the other side that all is well. It also reaffirms their view of you as an honest broker.

If in any doubt, or anything is unclear, never hold back from seeking clarification. Remember ambiguity breeds discontent, and the ability to recognize when to ask for more clarity is a vital part of reaching consensus. Generally, your opponent will be reassured that he is being listened to, and that that listener is taking a real and engaged interest in what he is saying. Even if none seems to be called for, it's a good idea to read the proposal and the draft contract, and ask yourself if everything looks clear. If it doesn't, make sure you raise any concerns before the negotiation itself takes place.

Stage Four: bargaining

To *bargain* means 'to negotiate the terms and conditions of a transaction', and appears here as a specific stage in the wider process of *negotiation*, 'to obtain or bring about by discussion'. Bargaining marks the climax of all the preparations, the planning and the mastery of skills – from observing to questioning, problem solving to strategizing. As the pivotal act in this drama, bargaining has a whole chapter to itself (chapter 7).

Avoid opening with extreme positions – you will alienate your counterpart before you've even begun. Instead, adopt an opening position that works for you yet manages the other side's expectations. Then aim to hold that position, as near as possible, throughout the process to closing.

Use the knowledge, insights and market intelligence you have gathered to gauge a realistic opening position and plan to concede a minimum to get the deal through and end with both sides content. Work out in advance those variables that are not so valuable to you, and flag these for potential 'sweeteners'.

Stage five: closure and implementation

We'll discuss at length the crucial business of closing in chapter 9. But ahead of time, before you have even embarked on proper negotiations, there are some further steps you can take to shore up your eventual success.

Always try to deal directly with the person most qualified to sign the deal. First, make sure you know who the decision maker is, and that they are not sending someone else on their behalf on more of an investigative mission. If this is the case, it's probably best to schedule the actual negotiation for a later date, and treat this investigative or discussion meeting as a more informal preamble. But do what you can to set up the meeting with the top person, the decision maker who has the power to grant what you're looking for.

Second, be realistic. Both sides should have already fathomed that the other is being genuine and clear, and is reputable. Otherwise they would have found some way out by now. To help things on their way, and especially as the deal itself comes more clearly into sight, try not to come across as too calculating. This could put the other side off.

At the same time, show you are prepared and have done your research. They will understand that a little knowledge is a dangerous thing, and will almost certainly have undertaken the same probing on you.

Third, create a real sense of momentum. Give your opponent a deadline for the proposed deal, and an incentive to commit to it. Make them feel you are giving them a real opportunity – one that is only available in this timeframe.

Sometimes you can turn their own time constraints to your advantage. I once found myself in the Middle East, trying to set up a book project with a tourism ministry. The contract was drafted, the minister was available and we set a date. After waiting around for most of the morning (the passage of time is sometimes not seen as important or even noticed in Middle Eastern culture), the door swung open, and we set to discussing the deal at hand. The afternoon passed and we had still not struck gold. He wanted guarantees the books would arrive unscathed (no mean feat in Yemen), and I sought tighter payment terms with a down payment to help us create the book. The minister suddenly pointed to a briefcase by his desk and told me he was flying to Riyadh that evening and we would have to continue our discussions another time. Politely protesting, I then took him by surprise and said, 'I'm coming with you to the airport.' I had no intention (nor a visa) to go to Saudi Arabia, but by the end of three hours sipping sharp Yemeni coffees in the departure lounge, I had the signed and stamped contract in my hands and could board my own flight back to London the next day, mission accomplished.

The moral of this story is, of course, that time constraints can in fact be excellent leverage. Try to use limited time to your advantage, and get the deal signed.

Finally, by way of last-minute preparation, sit down with a colleague who's familiar with the proposed deal and brainstorm any objections, valid or otherwise, the other side might raise. Come up with solutions or decent explanations for each. Tom Searcy, a sales adviser, calls this a 'landmine map' which details any anticipated stumbling blocks and problem areas.[23] Role play your sales pitch with your colleague and see what they come up with. It could be that, even by the eleventh hour, you have overlooked something critical.

Now all that's left is to make it happen.

6:

CULTURAL DIFFERENCES

Just because they're not on your road doesn't mean they've gotten lost
– Dalai Lama[24]

To travel is to discover that everyone is wrong about other countries
– Aldous Huxley[25]

As you'll have realized by now, negotiations are rarely easy things to tie up. (That's why so many people read books like this one.) With two sides to consider and a host of some-times competing interests, there is plenty of scope for lines of negotiation to get caught up in tangles. When you add to this the confusion and misunderstandings that cultural dif-ferences can bring, the potential for knots on a Gordian scale is massively increased. The myriad interpretations, approaches and behaviours combine to make international and cross-cultural negotiations much more complex affairs. In today's global marketplace, with its high levels of techno-logical integration, international negotiations are of course entirely commonplace. We take it for granted that we can set up a conference call from London with a business partner in Sydney and a client in Shanghai. We travel the world without a second's thought. The world's first non-stop flights are now operating between Sydney and London every day: a twenty-two-hour odyssey that brings those two centres that much closer together.

On a smaller scale, some ten trains hurtle non-stop through the Channel Tunnel every day (from where, as it happens, I am writing this chapter), bringing travellers to London and Paris in a little over two hours. Look beyond travel, and almost every business is so international as to be uniformly multi-ethnic. At my current company in London, we employ people of twelve different nationalities, speaking almost as many languages. We live in multicultural times, and this blending of cultures and ideas is every bit as enriching to the world of business as it is elsewhere in life.

Crossing cultures

Of course, international business deals not only cross borders, they cross cultures. Culture has profound implications for the way people think, behave and communicate. Consider this example from the website Negotiation Across Cultures:

> When Enron was still – and only – a pipeline company, it lost a major contract in India because local authorities felt that it was pushing negotiations too fast. In fact, the loss of the contract underlines the important role that cultural differences play in international negotiation. For one country's negotiators, time is money; for another's, the slower the negotiations, the better and more trust in the other side.[26]

To enter into formal negotiations is to be in a bubble where every interaction can have much greater impact and therefore carries more weight than it would in more normal situations. A negotiation is a mode of communicating whereby every gesture and utterance has heightened significance.

As with other hazardous areas, some preparation in advance can make a big difference to smoothing things over. Take time to learn about the culture with which you're planning to negotiate. Read around their traditions, society and etiquette. Try to establish how formal they are as a people, and which pitfalls you should be alert to. A good idea is to find another contact from that culture of whom you can ask questions. This will give you valuable insights into what your experience of negotiating within that culture will be like. Equip yourself with a certain amount of knowledge beforehand, and you should be able, quite literally, to negotiate your way around the world.

Travel

Travelling to negotiate is one of the most exciting events in many people's careers. It can be the height of adventure, and the apex of often otherwise drawn-out discussions. The thrill of being in a foreign culture – with all the challenges that entails; the new experiences and the prospect of 'mission accomplished' – is hard to beat. You'll need all the skills, knowledge, and preparation that come to bear in negotiations back home, and more.

By their very nature, all business trips are hectic. Time is money, and you will need to be as cost-effective as possible. As ever, be prepared. Check if you need a visa and send your application in early. Some embassies will take the best part of a month to process these.

Negotiating on foreign turf is also to put yourself at a potential disadvantage. You'll already be bargaining in the location of your opponent's choosing – probably their company boardroom or similar. Add to that the complexities of being in a professional setting in an alien environment, and the odds could well be stacked against you.

One of the first rules of business travel is to observe local customs and etiquette: you do not want to offend your host. Another good tip is to take things slowly at the first meeting. This can work to mutual benefit, as their comprehension of English might not be as good as it appears. This more measured pace will allow you to gather your thoughts and remind yourself of the various, often subtle, behaviours that will probably not be coming naturally you to at this stage – especially after a long-haul flight.

You may need to ask many different questions to adequately gauge the scope of the subject up for negotiation. It's good practice to do this as early as possible before sitting around the table. Give your opponent as much reasoning and background to your motive as possible. This way your opponent is likely to better understand your position, and why you are interested, and therefore be more open to sharing some information. This exercise, while often vital by way of a prelude to complex negotiations, also helps to foster a sense of mutual trust and respect – both all but essential if the process is to result in mutually favourable outcomes.

In many foreign countries, business cards play a much more important role than they do back home. Take plenty with you and consider getting some extras printed with the reverse in the local script. In some countries, such as China and Japan, this gesture can be especially appreciated. Across Asia, the giving and receiving of business cards (with both hands) is a formal exchange at the start of any business encounter, observed as standard.

When things go awry, remember you can always get help on the ground. Most international hotels have business centres with multi-lingual staff. They can be an invaluable help in printing last-minute name-cards, sourcing interpreters and helping with any travel arrangements. Your local embassy or consulate will list the chambers of commerce with offices in the vicinity. This list will include contact details of lawyers, advisers, tax advisers, shipping companies, trade organizations and the like.

Opportunities often arise when travelling in a foreign country. When they do, you may find yourself wanting to set up spontaneous meetings. In many non-English-speaking countries, the best way to do this is to recruit a local 'fixer' or agent to set up the meeting. In 2008, I was in Kazakhstan to set up a business traveller's handbook. My companion on the trip, Michael Fergus, a consultant from Norway, was researching the book, and in it he describes well the situation in Kazakhstan, perhaps one of the hardest places to do business I have ever encountered:

> A direct approach by a foreigner can be off-putting and is often met with refusal by a civil servant who is unsure of himself, or his fluency in English . . . If all else fails, it might be worth trying to get in without an appointment at all. That means convincing the security staff that you have an appointment when you do not and, if that works, it means trying to get the person you want to see to give you five minutes of their time there and then.

Practised business travellers usually know how to gate-crash as a last resort – and of course once the ice is broken things usually go swimmingly.[27]

One reason Kazakhstan is so complicated for the outsider is that the modern country is a mix of different influences and cultures. It is officially Kazakh-speaking, yet business is conducted in Russian with English a third language. It also blends its communist past with a recent embrace of capitalism, and often exhibits confusing aspects of both.

Different countries will present you with different challenges. The best advice is to brief yourself as thoroughly as possible before you touch down. Check out the immediate geography of where you're heading, get your bearings and pull up some local history. As well as being interesting in itself, this can go a long way to forming a bond with your host. Consider bringing a gift from back home. In some countries, such as Japan, this is customary, and seen as a polite way to open any formal meeting or negotiation. In other encounters, perhaps between Westerners, it can be viewed an attempt at bribery. Try to gauge the situation depending on the nationalities involved.

Figure out the value of the local currency – and which currency the contract is likely to stipulate. Often, the US dollar is used as a convenient and international meeting point. If a local currency is mooted for the deal, be careful to check its stability, and the exchange rate with your home or business currency. Dollars or euros are standard internationally accepted currencies. To some extent the British pound is too, but even though, at the time of writing, it has lost some of its value, it could still be seen as an expensive option to many foreigners.

Check to see if your would-be trip coincides with any national holidays. Some countries observe many more than others, and a day off could severely curtail your opportunities while there. Similarly, familiarize yourself with your host country's typical hours of business – and the working week. In Saudi Arabia, Iran and some other Muslim countries the working week is Saturday to Wednesday. Others go back to work on Sundays. Across the Islamic world, Friday is the day of rest and it is very bad form (or even forbidden outright) to work on that day.

Language

Language is the most obvious potential barrier to international negotiation. Even when both sides happen to speak with a common tongue, don't assume you won't encounter some culture-related difficulties. Help yourself along by avoiding trendy buzzwords, business jargon and colloquialisms. These will only add to your opponent's confusion. Take time to explain necessary technical terms, or contractual clauses. This will be appreciated, as will an effort to use simple phrases while doing so.

Even though we live in an age where the world's default business language is English, it remains highly likely that you will have instances where your counterpart cannot understand you, and vice versa. In such cases, you'll have little choice but to communicate using interpreters. Make sure you integrate your interpreter into your negotiating team – it's surprising how many people treat interpreters as outsiders, when in fact it's in their interests to keep interpreters onside. If effective, an interpreter can also work with you to overcome cultural differences. Remember, too, that you'll want to seal and sign the negotiations with the top decision maker, and this might not be the same person you've been talking to up until now.

Other forms of communication

When you don't share a common language with your host, you will often find there are many subtle, or less than subtle, differences in all types of communication. This could include figurative forms of speech, gestures and body language. You may also notice differences in the register, or mode of communication. Some business cultures value a more direct and simple dialogue, while others favour indirect and convoluted approaches.

This first, directness-valuing group includes Americans, Australians and Israelis. With these nationalities, you can generally expect clearer and more direct responses, and simple forms of expression. Others, such as the Japanese and Indians, are much more subtle and indirect in their dealings with others. Their responses and gestures can be hard to interpret, even vague. It will probably take time to reach a consensus, let alone formal commitment on a deal.

Style

The way people approach negotiations, and even meeting and greeting each other, is another variant the astute international negotiator studies carefully. In some cultures – Arab and some Asian for example – it can be difficult for a Western outsider to read the status of proceedings. When I was working in the Middle East, one of the greatest challenges was knowing when a proposal was no longer a proposition. Particularly with those from other cultures, Arabs often exhibit a reluctance to disappoint, so no one will ever tell you that in fact your wonderful idea for a deal is not to be. The directness of the Israelis versus the markedly different style of their Arab counterparts has arguably led to one of the most intractable negotiation stand-offs in history.

The confrontation of different styles of communication in the same negotiation can lead to friction. For example, the indirect ways in which Japanese negotiators express disapproval have often led foreign business executives to believe that their proposals were still under consideration when in fact the Japanese side has rejected them. In the Camp David negotiations that led to a peace treaty between Egypt and Israel in 1978, the Israeli preference for direct forms of communication and the Egyptian tendency to favour indirect forms sometimes exacerbated tensions between the two sides. The Egyptians interpreted Israeli directness as aggressiveness and, therefore, an insult. The Israelis viewed Egyptian indirectness with impatience and suspected them of insincerity, of not saying what they meant.[28]

In 2003, during the (ultimately failed) Six Party negotiations to rid the Korean peninsula of nuclear weapons, the Western negotiators were told not to smile as part of their brief. Whether or not this instruction contributed to the talks' eventual collapse, fully five years later, is worth considering. You would be hard pushed to find a culture anywhere in the world that didn't respond positively to good humour.

Diplomacy is about being prepared, and knowing what to expect and how to react. People associate diplomacy with politeness, but it can be tough-polite. It's always a good idea to under-promise and over-deliver.

Silence

Bill Coleman advises negotiators to count to ten. This, he says, 'is a gentle, soft indication of your disapproval and a great way to keep negotiating. Count to ten. By then, the other person usually will start talking and may very well make a higher offer.'[29]

As we discussed in chapter 2, when looking at essential skills, silence can be disconcerting for many people who grew up in a Western culture, and this can be turned to the negotiator's advantage. However, silence can be a perfectly normal part of discourse to those from other cultures. It's a common Western mistake when in Asia, for instance, to feel that silences must be filled. This often means the Western counterpart ends up hastily conceding something, while in fact the other side was turning over an idea, or about to suggest they order more tea, before continuing. It's a good idea to relax, and take things at the pace of your hosts.

Body language

Do you bow on first meeting? Should you use first-name terms? Do you shake hands? If your host keeps standing and walking around does this mean he is displeased? Can I blow my nose?

Body language, or what's commonly referred to as 'non-verbal communication', can be one of the most intimidating aspects of cross-cultural negotiations. A core skill required for negotiation is that of observing, or perception. Body language is no different. You should try to become a master of interpretation, and assume your opponent already is. Watch your own gestures, too, and maintain a good posture. You don't want to send the wrong signals.

In China I was often struck by how readily my hosts left the table to walk around the room before returning to their seat. In no way were they implying displeasure, let alone performing the emphatic 'walking away' negotiation technique. Two useful rules of thumb apply here. First, do your homework before you arrive. And second, take your cue from your host.

This second rule extends to something called 'mirroring', a trait also known as isopraxism. Have you ever noticed how groups of people on any given street tend to dress and talk alike? Or how some people start to speak with the accent of the person with whom they are talking? To some extent we all do it. We copy each other to create a sense of shared identity, which in turn we find comforting. We tend to fear what is different and are drawn towards what's similar, or familiar. This ingrained propensity to mirror each other is a biological principle, and it extends to everything, from how we dress to the phrases we use and the very tone of our voice (remember that question-sounding upspeak? It's especially prevalent in millennials). In business, and negotiation, the reasons behind mirroring are no different – we do it to establish some kind of rapport, which tends to lead to mutual trust.

In cross-cultural negotiations, particularly when you find yourself in the foreign city, you can consciously use mirroring to steer you through. Be careful, though, to use it with restraint. There's a fine line between taking your tone from someone, and mimicking them.

Punctuality

Time can prove to be a real dilemma for the business traveller. 'Time is money' is a well-known American phrase that speaks to the high value Westerners attribute to time in their cultures. Many other countries, too, place punctuality, in particular, in sacrosanct esteem. If you turn up late your business credentials can fall. Yet time is much less important across much of the Middle East and Africa. If you have an appointment in, say, Nigeria or Egypt, you should expect that negotiations will start rather later than planned. This is not due to the traffic (although this could very well cause either side to be later), but to a cultural indifference to punctuality that to the foreigner can be as frustrating as it is refreshing. I once waited three hours past our allotted time to see a minister in Yemen. When his retainer, who had been serving me tea in the interim, finally ushered me through, there was no mention of our late start, never mind an apology. Never take offence at such incidents, but try to adjust. Remind yourself that your way of doing things could seem just as strange to them. Some Arab countries along the Gulf, particularly the UAE and Qatar, have become more Westernized in their approach to time-keeping. But elsewhere, you should expect a more relaxed approach. In most Western countries, expect any tardiness to be frowned upon – regardless of traffic conditions.

Of course, the problem with business trips is that they usually come with tight schedules and, often, tight budgets.

In such situations, time really is money, and you might well have back-to-back meetings built in around the negotiation itself. You need to meet as many people as you can, in as little time as possible. Yet your hosts are not in the same hurry, and wider business patterns can be very casual. It is quite normal, for example, for business or negotiations in parts of Asia and the Middle East to be extended into lunch, dinner or even later. Whatever your schedule, you need to prioritize your negotiation meeting, as it is the reason you are there. If invitations arise for dinner, accept graciously – and worry about tomorrow's schedule in the morning.

Sometimes a limit on the time available to talk can work to the visitor's advantage. You can try to use the fact that in two days' time you have a plane to catch as method to try to focus your hosts on the matter in hand. Yet it's a fine balance: if you appear in too much of a hurry, you are vulnerable to going away empty handed. Or, if your opposite number knows you have one eye on the clock, he also knows you are likely to settle on his terms.

This is, then, the challenge of doing business in many other countries. You must give the impression to your opponent that you have all the time in the world, while quietly wondering how you're to get back to the hotel in time to pack for the flight. But, as with everything, the more you travel the easier such dilemmas are to overcome. And most accomplished negotiators take such challenges in their stride. Exceptionally, a deal could be so important that you've already resolved to stay in-country for as long as it takes, within reason (or at least until your visa runs out). One of my first foreign assignments was to Saudi Arabia. My boss handed me my ticket and pointed out it was one-way only, before walking away and with the words, 'Good luck,

Christopher. You won't be coming back empty handed.'
Quite literally.

Conclusions

It's worth, finally, summarizing some key tips that, together, should help shore up your success in any cross-cultural negotiations – wherever they might be.

1. Learn something about the culture in advance. Ideally, meet with someone who can informally explain some rules of the etiquette before you arrive.

2. Let the host side know in advance some of your key points. It helps to give them a call a day or two before your visit, followed with a summary email saying that you're looking forward to seeing them.

3. Regardless of any cultural or language barriers, try to stay calm, polite and focused on your strategy and the ultimate goal.

4. Try to be sanguine about the other side's behaviour. If they appear offensive, it is very likely that it is not intentional, and more of a cultural misunderstanding.

5. Always clarify when any hint of confusion emerges. Speak slowly and calmly, and if necessary ride those silences. Use simple language. Just expressing your willingness to learn can stand you in good stead.

6. Be a sensitive listener and ask appropriate questions. Remember that information is always power, and never more so than in a foreign culture.

7. Explain the key steps as you see them and invite your opponent to do the same. This reduces the scope for disagreement, or misunderstanding. Make sure both sides are aware of the agenda and what results they can expect.

8. Take care not to offend. Be polite, and if you're unsure about something, ask. Take your cue from your host – even with something as simple as sipping tea.

9. Be patient. Sometimes your host will expect the process to take a day or even several. This can allow time to get to know the other side, and also to test their trustworthiness, and build a stronger relationship. However slowly things may seem to be proceeding, never show any hint of impatience, let alone lose your temper.

10. Look the part: wear formal business attire, suit and tie for men. Take plenty of business cards and bring your brief and any other information you might need. Regardless of local tendencies, make sure you allow plenty of time for arriving at the allotted venue, bearing in mind unfamiliar streets and their traffic.

7:

THE DEAL

Let us never negotiate out of fear. But let us never fear to negotiate
— John F. Kennedy[30]

The best lesson I learnt from my father was how to negotiate
— Donald Trump Jr[31]

The big moment has arrived. You're finally on the cusp of making that deal, striking a bargain, clinching a raise, signing on the dotted line. Getting to this climactic stage, the 'real deal' as it were, is exciting, and ought to be fun. That handshake or flourish of signatures marks the start of something new, perhaps long hoped for, often in some real and significant way life changing. But the road to reaching that point of mutual consensus is fraught with hazards and obstacles, inhibitions and illusions. The route to agreement presents a nerve-wracking obstacle course for the uninitiated, an ordeal for the naïve and can end in disaster for the ill prepared.

So how to avoid these pitfalls? Ideally you'll first read chapter 5 of this book (which sets out the key stages: preparation and planning, defining the rules, clarification and problem solving, bargaining, closure and implementation). If you've read chapter 5, continue reading.

Even with the right level of awareness, knowledge and mental preparation, there is always a risk that things can go wrong. And when they do, they are more likely than not to go wrong in the final stages, and irreparably. Having come this far, it's important to keep reminding yourself of the eight core tenets set out in earlier chapters:

- Keep calm

- Be patient

- Stay focused

- Work to eliminate ambiguity or misunderstanding

- If necessary, buy time

- Remain in control of your emotions and your body language

- Be firm and clear while avoiding aggression

- If it feels unreasonable, or irresolvable, walk away

Before sitting down at the negotiating table, the most important point is to decide on a break-even point (the lowest amount or value you are prepared to accept). Then, once seated at the table, you then set the negotiations to open at the maximum sustainable position (the highest you can logically argue for or justify). These two figures form your parameters within which the discussions will take place. If all goes to plan, the negotiation process will move from your opening positions to somewhere nearer break even. In integrative negotiation, both sides will feel broadly satisfied.

How to pitch

Pitching is the climax of all negotiations, the moment when all that preparation risks being forgotten, when the pressure is building and those sound arguments get fumbled at best, or forgotten at worst. As such, pitching can be a nerve-wracking experience. Put simply, the pitch is a sale. At the very least, you're selling an idea, or an argument. You could be pitching for a pay rise or a new international trade deal; whatever the subject matter at hand, the same core principles apply.

First among these is an ability to maintain a studious anticipation. If you can accurately identify your opponent's threshold, you'll increase the likelihood of avoiding conflict. Remember the desired outcome is to agree to disagree, to some extent at least, and not to disagree to disagree. Through studying your opponent, allow your 'cushion' somewhere above your break-even point to rise or fall slightly depending on what they are revealing. Remember the 'bolstering range' (see page 61).

Secondly, know the value of your anticipated outcome. Base this on your research findings and also on the leverage you have. It's useful to have in mind a scale of pole positions and try to gauge where your situation falls on a scale of one to ten, where one is working to secure the release of a hostage (very weak) and ten is selling rare precious stones (very strong).

Take your time. Patience and a calm persistence are necessary to outlast your opponent. Keeping calm (at least on the outside) is reassuring to your opponent and gives the impression you are in control of your thoughts and your strategy, and that you are remaining focused on the goals you've set. Taking your time will really will help you to collect your thoughts in readiness for your next step. This is also why you should plan your proposal thoroughly and structure it well in advance, so you can maintain your trajectory, calmly in control of this process, that started when you sat down to figure out why you wanted this deal in the first place.

Then, aim high. If at all possible, try to get the other side to go first (remember the Istanbul bazaar?). But if not, don't shy from stating the highest value that your research says you can achieve. You don't expect to achieve this outright, but in contrast to pitching too low, you shouldn't come away disappointed, and certainly not empty handed. From this point on, always and only talk about your figure, the number you have in mind, and not theirs. By talking about the other side's numbers, you immediately lend them a certain legitimacy. You validate their sets of figures, and you lend your opponent a sense of confidence. And this is to give them the upper hand.

Having opened high, offset your climb-down by broadening the deal. You know they recently opened an office in China, but lack distribution. You could help them with this. Their campaign launches in September, and this month is looking quiet: you can work with them then, but after that is looking more difficult.

Next, and if appropriate, offer some concessions. But NEVER give away without getting something in return. Letting something go free of charge, as it were, is a big sign of weakness, and a lack of business acumen. Your opponent will then work to winkle more concessions, and you will come away the poorer.

Be alert to opportunities to seek something that is valuable to you but not worth so much to your opponent. Be open as to why you would like this, and what you could give in return. Building in 'barters' as part of the wider deal is common. Examples can include sharing technology platforms, reducing costs by sharing product distribution networks or media partnering to advertise each other's firms in different markets. Each side gains, and the gain can be greater for one than the other. It doesn't matter.

A useful method of bringing two sides closer to a final deal is to offer to pay upfront. Sometimes a longer, drawn-out contract with several stages over as many months lends itself to a system of staged payments. But in others, an upfront payment can make the difference between a deal and no deal. Paying upfront is not without risk, of course, but the benefits to getting on with the project often dispel any doubts. The very gesture bespeaks trust and the basis of a good working relationship.

Remember to avoid telling the other side *why* you are choosing them over their competitors. This sharing of knowledge can put them at an advantage (and it is largely irrelevant to the discussion at hand). Instead, focus on talking about how you want to do business with them.

What to ask for

Very simply, ask for what you want. But you should be confident you can get it. Your requests should be realistic and be made of a suitable partner who has the capacity to deliver. They need to come across as fair and reasonable. What you're asking for is essentially the goal you identified at the outset. Yet the reality of the negotiation table is that this will evolve in the course of discussions into something different. As bargaining progresses other, related, requests might come into play. For example, you might enter into discussions for a licence to trade in a free zone. Then, in the course of negotiations, it becomes clear that the most favourable terms hinge upon having warehousing in that free zone also. So you're now making two requests, and could reasonably expect to get a better overall deal as a result.

Countenance

Keeping a cool, calm and collected exterior is also a tactic to curb your enthusiasm. Essentially, to be an effective negotiator, you need to develop a heightened sense of self-awareness. How you react, look, move and speak will be giving signals to your opponent about your levels of comfort, confidence, ability and prowess. Control how you express yourself in order to send your opponent the message you want them to receive. Paring down your emotion, but not eliminating it altogether, is important. This way you avoid coming across as aloof or cold. No one wants to deal with someone who is not, at least in some way, engaging. It's a balancing act: be too emotional and your opponent will read you with ease. Too dour, and they'll find it hard to engage with you. Self-control and awareness are the watchwords. Learning to remain calm and be in control of your emotions will also help you to stay focused on your goals, and to make on-the-spot decisions with a cool head.

There are some tricks you can play. If it's not going well, you could even extend this to feigning boredom. Alternatively, looking nonplussed can leave your opponent feeling decidedly awkward. This in turn can undermine their confidence in their own pitch, and so the strength of their negotiating position dwindles. But this is the exception to the rule. In normal circumstances, try to maintain eye contact, instead of rolling your eyes and yawning.

Most importantly, act like you can make the deal work. Have a good attitude, and be positive throughout. Try not to lose sight of the fact that, once the contract is signed, you're going to be working with these people. So leave a good impression.

The contract

Almost every significant deal is backed up by a written contract of one sort or another. It's very important this document is given careful thought – all you've worked for up until now could be lost if the key agreements are not set out properly in a legally enforceable document. A contract's role is to bind the two parties in formal agreement, and to reflect accurately the role of either side in fulfilling that agreement. So it is perfectly normal for a contract to be redrafted several times before the negotiations are finalized and the papers are signed.

Once in its final form, the contract will clarify the identity of the parties, and who is to do what, by when. Payment stages and penalty clauses must be set out clearly. Sometimes these are listed in an appendix, but it doesn't really matter where they are, so long as they are written in the contract somewhere. The contract should set out any 'extras', and specify when these are to be delivered, and by whom. Exceptionally, unforeseen obstacles may force the amendment of the original contract. In such cases, an addendum is added by way of an extra page explaining, say, the mutually agreed later delivery dates. This, like the main body of the contract, should be signed and dated by both parties.

Many seasoned negotiators, far from relying on their own instincts and experience, use lawyers to finalize the contract every time they secure a deal. For other negotiators, a variation on a standard, in-house contract template will suffice. It depends on the scale of the negotiated deal, the importance to you, and how far removed it is from the day-to-day business you are already familiar with. Using the services of a lawyer is, of course, costly. But this is as nothing to the time and money lost should a major deal fall through at the eleventh hour. There are two immediate risks to using a lawyer to verify the contract: they are hired by the other side, and they slow things down. The pros and cons of using a lawyer should be weighed on a case-by-case basis.

Whether you choose to hire a lawyer or not, ensure you have a thorough record of the proceedings to date, with annotated agreements on the key points arising from the negotiations. These will form the basis of the contract. Don't be tempted to rush the final redrafting of the contract – it's too important. If extra time is needed to finish it properly, so be it. By this stage, most people just want to get it over with. But remember it's this document that will form the basis of your working relationship – signing it is just the beginning. So summon up your remaining reserves to work out a good contract. You'll save yourself a lot of hassle further down the road.

Conflict

The contract, if properly drawn up, serves to keep post-negotiation conflict to a minimum. Until it's finalized and signed there's plenty of scope for things to go wrong. In just the same way as you should tamp down your enthusiasm, so you should also train yourself to limit the risk of conflict. Conflict poses a great threat to negotiation, particularly in the later stages of discourse, and awareness of conflict risk, pre-emption and, if necessary, resolution is essential.

There are various reasons as to why conflicts arise within negotiations, but typically the conflict may exist because of ambiguity over responsibility and authority, competition over control of the situation, differences in work ethic or attitude, communication problems, personal or value-oriented differences and unequal reward systems.

Chief among causes of conflict is ambiguity. You should strive to eliminate any hint of ambiguity in the opening stages of negotiating. Ambiguity leads to confusion over power and authority, over which side holds responsibility for which areas under discussion, and tends to be at the heart of misunderstandings and communication problems.

A lack of preparation fuels ambiguity, so sound preparation goes a long way to reducing the chance of conflicts arising. In the run-up to the negotiation itself, talk to the other side frequently and work at building the foundations of a relationship. Picking up the phone is a great way to clear up misunderstandings. The sound of someone's voice is also a reassurance – they will feel they are getting to know you, and you will present yourself as on-side, on the ball and trustworthy. Do not rely on email alone.

Expectations should be similarly aired at an early stage.

Put your cards on the table at the outset. Make sure you're clear where the boundaries lie. During the negotiation itself, refer back to areas of common ground and work out from there. Perhaps there are variables on which both sides are willing to concede ground.

Other barriers to conflict resolution include psychology, ingrained perceptions, or even prejudices. Sometimes pre-conceptions – even from childhood – can get in the way. Sometimes these are cultural. In Arab countries, for instance, there is a heightened desire to avoid conflict in business at all costs – sometimes at the cost of logic itself. Be alert to this in international negotiations, and make an effort to clarify the key points early on, and ask the other party to do the same. Sometimes if everything appears just fine, and there is no cause for concern . . . you should be very worried indeed! Address any problematic issues with alacrity, and never negotiate in a fool's paradise.

Causes of conflict

The single greatest cause of conflict is lack of communication. Our email-driven business environment is particularly prone to this. Some things are simply better discussed face to face or, if that's not possible, over the phone or via Skype, Duo or similar platforms.

Yet there are some types of negotiations that are more prone to conflict than others. The first of these are family firms, often called family offices. Family members will often try to avoid conflict, rather than confront its causes. At some point, the cause becomes unavoidable, and the conse-quences can be painful. Several of Hong Kong's wealthiest families are currently embroiled in fierce disputes. The Lo family has decamped into two opposing sides in its fight for control of a $16bn trust fund, and resolving the issue appears all but impossible. This is partly because the passions and emotion that drive so many family relationships have spilled over into the boardroom – where there is a lot at stake.

Sound research can pre-empt that other frequent cause of conflict: cultural misunderstandings. Unintended misinterpretations have led to many a deal falling through – entirely unnecessarily. I once embarked upon negotiations with a Middle East client and entirely misread their timeframe. Assuming the deal was off (and that they were simply reluctant to tell me this), I thanked them and left. Two years later they came back, ready to do business. Thankfully, most deals do not normally take so long, but be aware that other people will do things differently (see chapter 6 for more on cultural differences and how to manage them).

Conflict can easily arise through the emergence of an imbalance of power – perhaps because one party tries to assert its dominance at the other's expense. The most entrenched examples of this kind of conflict can crop up in the unlikeliest of industries, such as book publishing. For most of 2013, the publishing house Simon & Schuster was, as the *New York Times* described it at the time 'locked into disagreement'[32] with America's biggest bookstore, Barnes & Noble. The latter had set out new terms to publishers, trumping the advantages that exposure in its many stores gives their titles. Simon & Schuster refused to play ball, and the bookseller in turn sharply reduced the number of their titles it was ordering. It took months of on-off negotiations to see the conflict resolved. The moral of this tale is: recognize your positions of power, but apply your leverage with great care, or your perceived aggression will harm both parties.

Conflict resolution

Conflict resolution can take various forms, including passive kinds, such as avoidance of the issue when one person allows the other to make the ultimate decision. Regardless, conflict resolution in its many forms is an imperative tool in having productive negotiation periods that ensure an objective will be met.

As we've seen, the ideal negotiating scenario is that two people maintain a trajectory towards securing a mutually beneficial agreement. But it is very common for both sides to disagree on the best way to reach that objective. As such, even passive forms of conflict resolution are essential to understand. In short, the ability to resolve conflict is a vital tool for ensuring effective negotiation.

Here, then, are four tried-and-tested conflict resolution strategies:

1. Separate interests and values by looking at the problem and each of the issues as part of a shared approach around the negotiating table. Try to ascertain what your opponent attaches to his various positions, as a way to break the impasse.

2. Try building relationships through a common cause or sense of rapport. Engage your counterpart by asking him to explain his positions and values.

3. Focus on shared values first, to help bridge any divide. This will bring you and your counterpart closer, by identifying mutual areas of interest. Using integrative negotiation strategies, you can establish some common ground, and then begin rebuilding areas of value to both parties.

4. Don't let differences between you fester. If you and your opponent fail, for whatever reason, to see eye to eye, try to work within areas of common ground first, and view areas of discord as opportunities you can revisit later in the process.

Even in cases where resolution of a dispute is impossible, these four lines of approach should result in greater understanding between the parties and help to clarify where the differences lie. In many cases, however, following the above steps will help ensure that a values-based dispute can be successfully negotiated.

Everyone's response to conflict within negotiations varies. According to the Foundation Coalition, there are five ways that people respond to conflict: through competition, compromise, avoidance, collaboration or accommodation. Each of these five response styles can be completed through assertiveness or cooperation. While the Foundation Coalition states that there are no 'wrong' modes of response, it counsels that 'there are right and wrong times to use each'. If you are managing negotiations between a team of people, assess each situation individually and decide what type of response style is best to adopt.

Certain barriers may lie in the path to effective conflict resolution. These barriers include how you view yourself and others, what you expect following the resolution of the conflict and what position of power you hold in relation to the person you are negotiating with. Gender can also act as a barrier, since the way certain people are taught to deal with conflict as a child may resurface in their adult years during negotiations. These barriers will not stop the resolution of conflict entirely, but can slow down the process and be difficult to navigate around. The differences can manifest themselves in significant ways. Men, for instance, tend to be more concerned with status (and the preservation of it) than women. Women, on the other hand, are often better at cultivating understanding, while their male counterparts could come across as more competitive. This is an area, of course, that suffers from stereotypical labelling, but it is nonetheless worth acknowledging by way of a quasi-cultural barrier.

Mediators

As something of a last resort, you could consider appointing a trusted third party to help overcome conflicts. Bringing someone else into the negotiations requires careful thought, though. The first challenge is they need to be neutral, and an acceptable ombudsman to both parties. Despite its advocacy from some, there is surprisingly little evidence mediation really works. And it tends to be the case anyway that parties who opt for some form of mediation are more willing to settle to begin with than parties who did not. It might be that your firm or organization has a particular area of business that is prone to disputes and conflicts. In this case, it makes sense to use a tried-and-tested mediator to help you resolve such differences.

Whether you choose to hire a mediator or not, ultimately the assessment of any risks falls to you. Ask yourself how intractable do the conflicts seem? Are you both pushing for things that can perhaps be dispensed with, or left for another time? Sometimes the most practical solution is to deliberately leave some items unresolved, and move ahead with the more certain aspects. In business as in wider life there are few certainties, so go with what feels workable, and avoid negativity.

Time and timing

As with all other forms of work, negotiations expand to fill the time available. We may not like to make important decisions under pressure, but deadlines can provide a healthy incentive to closing the deal. It's no accident that lawsuits settle on the steps of the courthouse and that strikes so often are averted the day before the picket lines are drawn.

A firm deadline should be established at the outset of negotiation. To avoid getting bogged down in never-ending talks, and as long as the other party does not feel they are being put under undue pressure, this is a good discipline to observe. You'll be able to move more quickly towards a resolution, and leave less time for problems to set in.

When to walk away

In walking away, you're not necessarily closing the door on negotiations. As a tactic, employed rarely, it can work with great effect. A friend of mine was once offered a promotion, and told that the board really wanted it to be him who filled the role. Great, except the new role was going to mean much more work and responsibility, managing the company's sales – all on the same salary. He politely pointed out that, with the sales manager gone, he would in effect be doing three people's jobs, and his boss offered a 3 per cent rise.

Offended, and disappointed, but seeing the talks were going nowhere, he suggested he would, in fact, be better off continuing with his current job instead. Saying he would consider his options, he politely rose, and walked out of the boardroom. The next day, he wrote to his boss to decline the offer of the new role altogether. Two weeks later, his boss came back admitting he had 'come around to his way of thinking'. My friend secured a 37 per cent pay rise. Quite a step up from 3 per cent.

My friend was ultimately successful. But be warned: walking away is the probably the most overused tactic in negotiation. And nine times out of ten, there is no going back. Professional negotiators even have an acronym for it: the Best Alternative to a Negotiated Agreement, or BATNA. The problem with walking away is that it's a tactic easily enacted by anyone, but the consequences can be disastrous. With the benefit of hindsight, it's probably safe to assume rather fewer would have embraced walking away.

The *Harvard Business Review* says that, as a source of relative power, walking away can 'help negotiators establish minimum or maximum thresholds beyond which a deal with a particular negotiator is of no value.'[33] The lower figure in the bolstering bracket we've spoken of as part of our strategy is often referred to as the 'walk-away' figure, or breaking point. Negotiations beyond this line are taken as futile. Don't forget that, right at the outset, you established certain boundaries within which you would strike a deal.

If you do find yourself bargaining for a deal that seemingly cannot meet your lowest goal, then you have little choice but to walk away. Preface by clearly explaining to your opponent your position and the reasons why you cannot accept their offer, thank them for their time, and courteously leave the room. In this way the door is (metaphorically at least) left ajar should the other side have second thoughts (and they often do), and wish to come back. But in the majority of cases you need to accept the win-some-lose-some nature of business and move on. Any loss of face you suffer in walking away from a bad deal is as nothing to the embarrassment of having to explain to your board why you signed on for the thing. As one Donald Trump once put it, 'Sometimes your best investments are the ones you don't make.'[34]

Remember, negotiation results in a longer-term commitment with consequences you will have to live with. So if it doesn't seem right, or it's not what you want, you're better off not signing up for it. People can sometimes be so caught up in the process of negotiation itself, they can actually lose sight of the fact that it is merely the first step in a much longer working relationship. Signing up for a bad deal is far worse than having no deal at all.

Very occasionally, you might find yourself up against a side that has little respect for the truth, or that your instinct tells you is fundamentally untrustworthy. Perhaps they are trying to persuade you to enter into other deals on the side, and you feel undue pressure. In these, rare, instances, you should not walk away but rather run!

Closing the deal

When it comes to closing the deal (if it's still on, that is) be sure to confirm that all the key points have been covered so there will be no last-minute surprises. It's surprising how many people try to append something onto the deal at the last minute, even after a firm handshake. We all know that when the car salesman disappears to clear your price with his boss, that he'll be back with bad news. But surprises in negotiation are poor form and bad practice. Neither proffer nor accept such low tactics.

This aside, there are typically two forms of closing. You are either concerned with bringing differing ideas to a coherent and mutually agreed conclusion, or with how to formalize that agreement. Whichever, try to think of closing as a process to gaining validation or acceptance, as opposed to forcing agreement on your opposite side. What you want is for both parties to 'buy in' to the agreement: the 'win-win' outcome of integrative negotiation.

Sometimes you can sense the other side is close to a deal but needs one final push. For example, if you're a broker and your client is scheduled to buy this coming week regardless of this seller's role, this is a strong closing argument. The other side is reminded of the time constraints if they want to join the deal – and this could be a deciding factor. It's different from asking for something more and is a genuine attempt to bring all sides to a conclusive, constructive agreement.

Remember, too, all that research you did in the earlier stages, and use it to your advantage. *Harvard Business Review* cited the following case study, which I quote here in full by way of illustrating the role information can play in this process:

A couple of years ago [2013], two cofounders of a tech venture walked into a meeting with the CEO of a *Fortune* 100 company who had agreed to invest $10m with them. A week earlier, the parties had hammered out the investment amount and valuation, so the meeting was supposed to be celebratory more than anything else. When the cofounders entered the room, they were surprised to see a team of lawyers and bankers. The CEO was also there, but it soon became clear that he was not going to actively participate.

As soon as the cofounders sat down, the bankers on the other side started to renegotiate the deal. The $10m investment was still on the table, but now they demanded a much lower valuation; in other words, the cofounders would have to give up significantly more equity. Their attempts to explain that an agreement had already been reached were to no avail.

What was going on? Had the cofounders misunderstood the level of commitment in the previous meeting? Had they overlooked steps involved in finalizing the deal? Had the CEO intended to renege all along – or had his team convinced him that the deal could be sweetened?

Upset and confused, the cofounders quickly assessed their options. Accepting the new deal would hurt financially (and psychologically), but they'd get the $10m in needed funds. On the other hand, doing so would significantly undervalue what they brought to the table. They decided to walk out without a deal. Before they left, they emphasized their strong desire to do a deal on the initial terms and explained that this was a matter of principle as well as economics. Within hours, they were on a plane, not knowing what would happen. A few days later, the CEO called and accepted the original deal.[35]

A dangerous trap to avoid in the closing stage (and people are especially prone to it when tired) is to assume that every concession the other side has made was insignificant: 'they didn't really want it anyway'. Avoid this negative way of thinking: it will not end well. Instead, recognize their concessions for what they are, and work to get them to accept some of yours also. Remember that what's valuable to you might genuinely be worth less to them, and vice versa.

Amid all the focus on the present, look again at the contract before you sign. People often forget to pay sufficiently close attention in the final stages, and in particular to check that the phrasing of the exit clauses is conducive to re-negotiating the deal in future.

If, after all that, you have secured that win-win agreement, shake hands, congratulate the other side, thank them and relax. On the way home, turn over what you might have done differently, and what you did well. Above all, give yourself credit for what you've just achieved. You've mastered one of life's most useful and complex skills.

8:
CONCLUSIONS

Let every eye negotiate for itself, and trust no agent
– William Shakespeare, *Much Ado About Nothing*,
Act II, scene 1

In the course of my research for this book, I found myself from time to time making visits to the British Library. Arriving in the business section and finding shelves (there are many) dedicated to the subject of negotiation, I chose three books at random from the general negotiation guides shelf. The sub-headings made them sound much more exciting than the actual titles. 'How to get the best deal every time', one promised. The other vowed to teach you the art of 'Negotiating as if your life depended on it'. 'Your definitive guide to success' read another.

I looked down my list of ideas for how to structure my own book on negotiation, and my eye fell on my scribbled notes around the subject of closing. Flicking through to the index of each of the three titles in my hands, I wanted to see what others had said on this pretty crucial topic. It wasn't there. C. Closure. Closing perhaps. Maybe under Negotiation, final stages of, something like that. But there was nothing there either. How could this be?

My quest revealed something about this big subject: it is massively and unnecessarily overcomplicated. Those indices were peppered instead with apparent topics I had never heard of, such as 'the E factor', 'the clock face', and 'Mother Hubbard' (ten pages on that one). It seems everyone wants to coin an acronym or concept of their own, and give it a label. In so doing, each adds his own opaque layer to the many already wrapped around the subject, when, in reality, negotiation boils down to some pretty simple rules and stages. (E, by the way, stands for Emotion. I'll leave you to figure out what Mother Hubbard refers to.)

Many negotiated situations are highly complex – that's why you're there. The mistake is to extend that complexity to the negotiation process itself. Strive to keep the process as straightforward and clear as you can. In many ways, I would argue the greater the clarity and simplicity you can bring to the table, the better your chances of success. A good place to start is with a positive attitude. This sounds like an over-simplification – but it's true. And it really works. Being positive and demonstrating a positive attitude from the start can make an enormous difference to the outcome, as well as making the process that leads to the deal all the more pleasant for everyone. A positive attitude paves the way to a trusting relationship. Along the way:

- Prepare, prepare, prepare. Know who you're negotiating with and why they are there. Understand what's important to them, and work at ensuring some of their objectives are met, too.

- Identify common ground, and be prepared to concede in principle. But never give without getting something in return.

- Maintain frequent communications throughout. Form a good relationship with your opponent, even (especially) if you disagree.

- Remain calm and courteous, and never get upset, no matter how badly things might be going.

- Finally, look over that contract like a hawk!

Negotiation is a life skill like no other. It touches on many different disciplines, from strategizing to empathy and psychology. It works its way into our daily lives so pervasively we often cease to give it much attention. Yet its multidisciplinary nature, coupled with its sheer usefulness as a skill, makes it a fascinating subject in itself (which is probably why you've been bearing with me all this way). And its extraordinary potential lies with the fact that it only really works to good effect when there's a strong relationship at its heart. This is arguably the soaring achievement of all negotiation, in whatever sphere it takes place: successful negotiation symbolizes a triumph for the human capacity to collaborate, despite, or even because of, our differences. It means two people coming together – in any setting imaginable – in a spirit of optimism, and with a common goal in sight. At the height of its powers, negotiation can forge friendship between enemies, and peace from conflict. In business, negotiation is the medium that brings people together to make something happen; the catalyst behind every single contract. Its possibilities are unlimited, and unrivalled. Learning how to negotiate really is the greatest skill anyone can master. Good luck.

NOTES

1 Boye, H., *Selling Songs Successfully*, New York: Lifetime Books, 1995

2 Lewis Fernandez, E., *Think Like a Negotiator*, Irvine, CA, 2013

3 http://db.nelsonmandela.org/speeches/pub_view.asp?pg= item&ItemID=NMS013

4 https://www.psychologytoday.com/intl/basics/empathy

5 Eds. Rubin, Jeffrey Z., William Zartman, I., *Power and Negotiation*, University of Michigan Press, 2002

6 Kiam, Victor, *Going For It!: How to Succeed as an Entrepreneur*, London: HarperCollins, 1986

7 Morrow, L., 1939 –, Journalist and Essayist

8 Trump, I., *Time*, 3 February 2016

9 Camp, J., *Start with NO: The Negotiating Tools that the Pros Don't Want You to Know*, Crown Business, New York, 2002

10 Coleman, William "Bill" T. III, 1947–, Executive and Buisnessman

11 Kipling, R., *Selected Poems*, London: Penguin Classics, 1993

12 Koslow, B., *365 Ways to Become a Millionaire: (Without Being Born One)*, Plume, New York, 2007

13 Newsom, G., *San Francisco Chronicle*, 7th June 2011

14 Gadhia, A., 'Win your negotiation: How to research your opponent before the battle', *Technology Transfer Tactics*, November 2012

15 'It Pays to Know Your Opponent: Success in Negotiations

Improved by Perspective-Taking, But Limited by Empathy',
Psychological Science, 22 April 2008

16 https://www.pon.harvard.edu/daily/win-win-daily/win-win-
negotiations-managing-your-counterparts-satisfaction/

17 Mackay, H., *Swim with the Sharks without Being Eaten Alive:
Outsell, Outmanage, Outmotivate, and Outnegotiate Your
Competition*, Brighton: Ivy Books, 1988

18 http://www.cssp.com/CD0808b/CriticalStrategic
ThinkingSkills/

19 Lipman, J., *That's What She Said,* New York: William Morrow,
2018

20 Voss, Chris and Raz, Tahl, *Never Split the Difference,* London:
Penguin, 2016

21 https://www8.gsb.columbia.edu/newsroom/newsn/3497/
when-it-comes-to-an-opening-number-sometimes-the-best-
bargaining-move-is-to-offer-two

22 Stanley Judd, H. *Think Rich*, New York: Delacorte Press, 1978

23 https://www.inc.com/tom-searcy/how-to-close-deals-faster-
and-smoother.html

24 Dalai Lama, *Freedom in Exile: The Autobiography of the Dalai
Lama*, London: Little, Brown and Co., 1990

25 Huxley, A., 1894–1963, Author

26 Salacuse, J. W, 'Negotiating: The Top Ten Ways that Culture
Can Affect Your Negotiation', *Ivey Business Journal*,
September/October 2004

27 Fergus, Michael, *Kazakhstan, The Business Traveller's
Handbook,* London: Stacey International, 2009

28 https://www.skillsyouneed.com/rhubarb/negotiation-across-
cultures.html

29 Bottos, L. M. and Coleman, B., 'The New Salary Negotiation',
Compensation and Benefits Review, Vol 34, Issue 2, 2002

30 Kennedy, J. F., speech given before the UN General Assembly, 25 September 1961

31 Trump Jr., D., ep. 1, *Trump: An American Dream,* 72films, November 2017

32 Bosman, J., 'Simon & Schuster and Barnes & Noble Reach a Deal', *New York Times,* 19 August 2013

33 Hewlin, J. A., 'The Most Overused Negotiating Tactic Is Threatening to Walk Away', *Harvard Business Review,* 18 September 2017

34 https://twitter.com/realdonaldtrump/status/415361711529 787392?lang=en

35 Malhotre, D., 'Control the Negotiation Before It Begins', *Harvard Business Review,* December 2015

Index

acrimony, avoiding 27
acting 37–8
African National Congress (ANC) 11
agenda:
    drafting the 23
    motivation and 49, 50
aggression, avoiding 39, 40, 41, 84,
    92, 102
al-Assad, Bashar 11
ambiguity, eliminating 27, 34, 40, 72,
    92, 99
Annan, Kofi 11
Arab world 8, 11, 83–4, 87, 100 *see also*
    individual nation name
assertiveness 30, 40–1, 103
avoid, things to 26–8
    acrimony 27
    emotion 28
    greed 27–8
    price, their 26–7

Babcock, Linda 60
bargaining 64, 65, 72–3, 91
Barnes & Noble 101–2
bartering 12
Best Alternative to a Negotiated
    Agreement (BATNA) 106
body language (non-verbal
    communication) 31, 83,
    85–7, 92
bolstering range 61–2, 65,
    93, 106
boundaries, establishing 47
Boye, Henry 1
break-even point 92, 93
break-out sessions 59–60

Britain:
    Brexit and 9, 10
    negotiation culture in 7
business cards 79–80, 90
business plan 5, 55

calm, keeping 3, 30, 32, 38, 39, 89, 92,
    93–4, 96, 113
Camp David Accords (1978) 84
Camp, Jim: *Start with No: The*
    Negotiating Tools that the Pros Don't
    Want You to Know 32
Carnegie Mellon University 60
Center for Strategic Planning 53–5
Chandler, Raymond 61
China 8, 9, 11, 13, 25, 48–9, 69, 72–3,
    79–80, 86, 94
clarification:
    clarification and problem solving
    stage of negotiation 40, 64, 65,
    71–2
    seeking 40
closure and implementation 64, 65,
    73–5
Coleman, Bill 35, 85
Columbia Business School 61–2
common ground 6, 100, 112
compromise 1, 2, 14, 15, 18, 21, 39,
    41, 103
conflict 24, 25, 28, 72, 93, 99–105, 113
    causes of 100–2
    mediators and 104–5
    resolution 102–4
contract 67, 68–70, 81, 95, 97–8, 99,
    110, 113
control, taking 23–4

core tenets, negotiation 92
countenance 96–7
counter, always 59
Cuban Missile Crisis (1962) 6–7
cultural differences 7–9, 76–90
   body language 85–7, 92
   communication, forms of 83
   crossing cultures 77–8
   key tips 89–90
   language 82–3
   punctuality 87–9
   silence 85
   style, negotiations 83–5
   travel 78–82

Dalai Lama 76
deadlines 70, 74, 105
deal, the 91–110
   break-even point and maximum
      sustainable position 92
   closing 108–10
   conflict and 98–105
   contract 97–8
   countenance and 96–7
   eight core tenets and 92
   pitch, how to 93–5
   time and timing 105
   walk away, when to 105–7
   what to ask for 95–6
Deane, Silas 6
decision making 30, 36
de Klerk, F.W. 11–12
delivery 67, 68–9, 70, 98
diplomacy 2, 9–12, 84–5
distributive negotiation 12–13, 14, 57
Double Indemnity (film) 61
dynamics, understand the 58

eBay 56
ego, adult 39
Egypt 84, 87
emotions, controlling 28, 30, 38–9,
   92, 96
empathy 19–20, 31, 33, 44–5, 52–3, 113
Enron 77
European Union (EU) 9, 10
eye contact 31, 97

family, conflict and 100–1
Fergus, Michael 80–1
First World War (1939–45) 6
focused, stay 15, 37, 39, 89, 92,
   93–4, 96
Foundation Coalition 103
France 7
Franco-American Treaty (1778) 6
Frost, David 9

Gadhia, Ami 43
Germany 8
goodwill 41, 58, 62
Google 20, 45, 46, 51
greed, avoiding 27–8
Grevier, Charles 6

haggling 9, 12, 65
Harvard Business Review 106,
   108–9
Harvard Law School 63
Hong Kong 8, 46, 100–1
hostage crises 2, 4, 71, 93
hosting, negotiation 23–4
Huxley, Aldous 76

India 8–9, 77, 83
information, using 25–6
initiative 58
integrative negotiation 12, 13–14, 15,
   18, 57, 92, 103, 108
Iran 2, 8, 9, 82
   nuclear deal 2, 9, 10–11
Israel 83, 84

Japan 80, 81, 83, 84
Johns Hopkins University 43
Judd, H. Stanley 63

Kazakhstan 80–1
Kennedy, John F. 6–7, 91
Kerry, John 2, 10, 11
Kiam, Victor 29
Kipling, Rudyard: 'If' 38
knowing what you want 1–2,
   15, 52
Koslow, Brian 38

language, international negotiation and 82–3
leaving the negotiation *see* walking away
Lee, Arthur 6
letter of intent 59
Lewis-Fernandez, Eldonna: *Think Like a Negotiator* 14
listening 3, 30, 34, 54, 58
Lo family 101

managing expectations 22, 50
Mandela, Nelson 11–12, 17
maximum sustainable position 52, 92, 93
McDonald's 48–9
mediators 104–5
mirroring 86–7
Molière: *Tartuffe* 1
Morrow, Lance 29

negotiation:
  compromise, as art of 1, 2, 14, 15, 18, 21, 39, 41, 103
  cultural differences and 7–9, 76–90
  deal, the 91–110
  diplomacy and 2, 9–12
  distributive 12–13, 14, 57
  etymology 5–6
  integrative 12, 13–14, 15, 18, 57, 92, 103, 108
  life skill, as a 2–5, 17, 113
  misunderstood skill, as a 3, 29
  opponent, knowing your 42–50
  origins of 5–7
  power and psychology of 17–28
  skills, essential 29–41
  stages, key 63–75
  strategy 51–62
  types of 12–15, 18, 57 *see also individual type of negotiation*
Negotiation Across Cultures 77
Netherlands 7–8
Newsom, Gavin 42
Nigeria 87
North America 7
North Korea 9

Obama, Barack 10, 11
observe 29, 30–1
opponent, know your 3–4, 8, 23, 24, 29, 30–1, 42–50, 93, 112
  agendas and motivation 49
  boundaries, establishing 47
  managing expectations 50
  perspective taking 42–5
  research and 45
  what information are you setting out to find 46–7
  withholding information 48–9

Paris Peace Treaties (1947) 6
patience 54–5, 90, 92, 93–4
payment 67, 70, 74, 95, 97
PayPal 56
perspective taking 42–5
pitch, how to 93–5
positive attitude 41, 112
Potsdam Agreement (1945) 6
power *see* psychology, power and
preparation and planning 58, 64, 66–70, 91, 112
  contract 67, 69–70
  delivery 67, 68–9
  payment 67, 70
  pricing 67, 68
  volume/scale 67, 68
pricing 13, 26–7, 43–4, 49, 58, 59, 60, 65, 67, 68, 108
prioritizing 30, 36–7
problem solving 13, 30, 36, 57, 64, 71–2, 91
Psychological Science 43–4
psychology, power and 17–28
  avoid, things to 26–8
  control, taking 23–4
  information, using 25–6
  psychology of negotiation 18–20
  power, real and perceived 20–1
  states of mind, managing 21–3
punctuality 87–9

questioning:
  cultural differences and 79, 89
  research and 43

questioning (*cont.*)
  skill of 30, 33–4, 35, 36
  strategy and 59

Rayneval, Conrad Alexandre de 6
research 45
Russia 7, 11

salaries 27, 52, 60–2, 106
Saudi Arabia 74, 82, 88–9
Second World War (9349–45) 7
Shakespeare, William: *Much Ado About
    Nothing* 111
silence, using 29, 30, 34–5, 85
Simon & Schuster 101–2
Singapore 8, 9
Six Party negotiations, North Korean
    nuclear weapons (2003) 84
skills, essential 29–41
  acting 37–8
  assertiveness 30, 40–1
  clarifying 40
  decision making 30, 36
  emotions, controlling 30,
    38–9
  listening 30, 34
  observing 30–1
  positive attitude 41
  prioritizing 30, 36–7
  problem solving 30
  questioning 30, 33–4
  silence, using 30, 34–5
  speaking 30, 32
South Africa 11–12
speaking 30, 32
stages, key 63–75
  bargaining 64, 65, 72–3
  clarification and problem solving 64,
    65, 71–2
  closure and implementation 64, 65,
    73–5
  preparation and planning 64,
    66–70
  rules, defining the 64, 70–1
STaRs model (Start-up, Turn-around,
    Realignment and Sustaining
    success) 55–7

states of mind, managing
    21–3
strategy 51–62
  break-out sessions 59–60
  definition of 51–3
  implementation 55
  salaries 60–2
  STaRs model (Start-up, Turn-around,
    Realignment and Sustaining
    success) 55–7
  strategic thinking 53–5
  strategy with situation, aligning
    55–6
  tactics and 57–9
  types of negotiation for the
    strategy 57
style, negotiations 83–5
Sun Tzu: *The Art of War* 25
SWOT analysis 55
Syria 9, 11

tactics, strategy and 57–9
  counter 59
  dynamics, understand the 58
  goodwill 58
  initiative 58
  letter of intent 59
  listen 58
  preparation 58
  questions, ask 59
  time management 59
  walk away 59
Thant, General U 7
time/timing 24, 105
  deal and 92, 105
  management 59
  taking control of 24
tone, vocal 32
trade talks 9, 10, 13
travel, negotiation and 78–82
Trianon, Treaty of (1920) 6
Trump, Donald 9, 13, 107
Trump Jr, Donald 91
Trump, Ivanka 29

United Nations (UN) 7, 11
upspeaking 32, 33, 86

Veritas Technologies 35
volume/scale 67, 68
Voss, Chris: *Never Split the Difference*
    60–1

walk away value 13
walking away 13, 38–9, 48, 59, 86, 92,
    105–7, 109–10
Watkins, Michael D. 55, 56

weaknesses/threats, embracing 55
WIIFM (What's In It For Me?)/WIIFT
    (What's In It For Them?) 15
Wilder, Billy 61
withholding information 48–9, 64

Yemen 74, 87

Zartman, William 20